William Scoville Case

Forward house

A Romance

William Scoville Case

Forward house
A Romance

ISBN/EAN: 9783744664752

Printed in Europe, USA, Canada, Australia, Japan

Cover: Foto ©Thomas Meinert / pixelio.de

More available books at **www.hansebooks.com**

Forward House

IN UNIFORM BINDING.

FORWARD HOUSE. A Romance. By William Scoville Case.

A TRUCE, and Other Stories. By Mary Tappan Wright.

A MAN WITHOUT A MEMORY, and Other Stories. By William Henry Shelton.

MARSENA, and Other Stories. By Harold Frederic.

A POUND OF CURE. A Story of Monte Carlo. By William Henry Bishop.

TALES OF THE MAINE COAST. By Noah Brooks.

SALEM KITTREDGE, and Other Stories. By Bliss Perry.

** Each One Volume, 16mo. Price, $1.00.

Forward House

A Romance

BY

WILLIAM SCOVILLE CASE

NEW YORK

CHARLES SCRIBNER'S SONS

1895

TROW DIRECTORY
PRINTING AND BOOKBINDING COMPANY
NEW YORK

CONTENTS

v

Contents

Contents

FORWARD HOUSE

I

FOR the better part of my life I have lived by the sea, and the love I bore her as a boy has strengthened with my years. I love her dignity and the majesty of her anger, and I love her moods, for they are mine. But she has trusted me with no confidences, and has held me at arm's length. She has turned her gray face to me when I have fled to her, miserable and lonely, yet there is no happiness beyond the murmur of her voice. And though I am neither a sailor nor a sailor's son, and can see from my perch on the point rocks farther than a boat has ever carried me, I have often crept from my bed on dark nights, when the wind was rising and the surf boomed along the shore, and climbed the cliff to hear and feel the storm. And I have lain there sometimes, turning my cheek to the stinging slap of the spray, until morning shamed me and I slunk back, lest the sea should laugh at my weakness for her.

It is an almost forgotten coast here where I live alone—a narrow point of land that thrusts obtrusively out to sea, ignored by the railroads, shunned by commerce, and, I thank God, still unfound and unpolluted by the summer way-farer. The plot of ground that I call my own is meagre enough, but my house stands on a lonely stretch of road with the ragged end of the cape half a mile eastward, and the dead fishing village of East Crag as far behind the hill on the west, guarding the little bay on the north shore. A hundred yards behind my house the pines begin and cover the slope from there to the water-side nearly a mile away, while across the road before me is open ground, rising to the hill that skirts the southern coast of the cape, and here is a dense and untrimmed wood. No living creature, so far as I know, is kin of mine in our small sense of the word, and I have lived too long in the world to claim a broader kinship with the men about me. But I am on very good terms with my books, and I love the neighbors that Nature sends me to nest in my trees and burrow in my garden. I love them all, and they trust me. I love the woods and the smell of the earth, but more than all else, I love the sea.

From my front porch I can see both east and west along the disused road that was the trodden path of the hardy fishing folk to their lookout on the point when East Crag was a bigger place with ships at sea. All that is past now, and the road serves only me, as my avenue to the village when I have to go that way, and to the ocean when my mood draws me to her. From here I look to the sea's edge on one side, and to the crest of the hill where the road dives abruptly down into the village on the other. But my present house is not so artfully hidden by the trees and the shrubbery as the old one was, for when that was standing, no summer passer on the road would observe it even by day, unless he chanced to see the polished brass knocker of my front door flash through the leaves when the sun struck it. I used in those days to sit in absolute concealment on my front steps in the dark of summer evenings.

Late one August night I sat there smoking my pipe and listening to the restless grieving of the sea, when a light rose out of the darkness and flickered unsteadily on the crest of the village hill. It swayed gently to and fro to the motion of a rapid walker, and dropped slowly to the level of my eyes, so that I knew it for a lantern. Now and then it paled as a sudden gust of wind swept up the road, and once it disappeared altogether at a furious blast, as though the bearer had turned back to the wind and waited for the lull to follow. The action was significant, for it takes a mighty blast to turn an East Crag fisherman in his tracks, and I was not surprised when the light appeared again and the figure had come nearer, to see the skirts of a woman. Now travel by my house is rare enough by day, and there is none by night—still, a stray man by way of diversion would not have stirred me greatly even at that hour, but a solitary woman flitting noiselessly along the road at one o'clock in the morning, whose only conceivable destination was the lonely rock beyond, pricked my curiosity. She came on swiftly until about a hundred yards away, when she stopped, and lifting the lantern level with her face, turned down the light and hid the lantern in the folds of her skirt—so I knew she was no stranger to the place and meant to avoid observation from my house. The thing was quickly done, but in that instant, and even at that distance, my keen sight noted both her youth and the whiteness of her face. In the dark that followed, I bent my head to catch the rustle of her skirts as she passed, but I heard no sound save the thunder of the sea, and after an interval of waiting I saw her light sparkle again far along the road, and lessen as it zigzagged toward the cliff.

I cannot well describe the impression that the incident made upon me, and though I am loath to believe myself a greater coward than most men, I confess to no slight satisfaction at that moment that the woman's first thought was to avoid me. Whoever she was and whatever her mission, she had plainly some reason for concealment, and the fatal characteristic of her sex had shown in her compromising caution. Had she come in darkness, I had never known her presence, or had she even held boldly by her light, I dare say my curiosity would have waned with her passing, and I had given her no second thought. But the very act by which she courted secrecy, advertised her presence and set a seal of mystery upon it that I was not proof against. I laid aside my pipe, took up my hat, and followed her.

The moon had long ago gone down, and no stars were out. The night was dark, but I knew every inch of the road, and held my way in the teeth of the rising wind until I came to the foot of the cliff. The light was stationary now, pricking the gloom above me at the very edge of the sea, and I stopped to watch it. To tell the truth, I had no great desire to get to closer quarters, and when I realized that the woman had gone as far as she could, I was content to remain in the background. Indeed, as I stood there I began to feel an uncomfortable sense of shame. What business had I meddling with the matter? Had not I, of all men, learned my lesson too well for that? I even turned to retrace my steps, but I was arrested half-way by a movement of the light, which waved slowly from right to left twice. Before it had completed the second arc, I was startled by a sound in the road behind, and an instant later a man rushed past me so close that I could hear his breathing. I traced his stumbling progress up the hill, by the light beyond, which his body hid every now and then so that it looked like a star wading through cloud. Then I heard him hailing angrily as he came nearer it, and a woman's answering cry, and with that the light went out altogether and I heard and saw no more.

But I had lost my caution when the woman screamed, and was running madly up the hill, nor did I stop until something tripped me at the top, and I sprawled my length upon the turf.

6

I lay there listening and staring about me with eyes grown accustomed to the darkness, but I heard nothing above the roar of the wind and waves, and saw only the black outline of the wood against the sky, to one side, and the pale tops of the breakers fifty feet below. And then, as my eyes went seaward, I saw what chilled my marrow, for out of the wilderness beyond a light flashed again and waved slowly from right to left. Then it disappeared. For a moment I thought the woman had gone clean out to sea, but my reason came back to me when, after a little groping, I found what had tripped me, and it proved to be a lantern the metal of which was still hot. So putting two and two together, I realized that the last light had probably been an answering signal from some ship just off shore. With a burning curiosity, and without reckoning on the likelihood of a personal encounter with people whose business I was making my own, I began exploring the place in the dark. It was useless to try to relight the lantern in the fierce wind that was blowing, and I groped about on my hands and knees in a widening circle. On my second trip around, my hand closed upon a small bottle with a glass-stopper, and near it on the turf I hit upon a tobacco-pipe.

7

I do not now remember that I hesitated to appropriate this property, and I have often wondered since that I made no more ado about pocketing it. At any rate, I put both bottle and pipe away, and continued my search until I had almost fallen into the sea from going too near the edge of the cliff. Then I picked myself up, and with stolen property under my coat, thanked God for my narrow escape from drowning, and went my way unmolested. I stopped under the lee of the hill to light the lantern, and then set off for home. But I walked slowly, for I had wrenched my ankle by the fall I got, and I had just reached the level road again when a man seemed to rise up out of the ground at my feet. At that instant the wind swept down the road so strong that it nearly blew my light out and we could see each other only dimly. My heart beat rather high, for I thought I had come to a reckoning with the woman's pursuer, but the man's first words reassured me and showed me my mistake.

" For God's sake," he shouted angrily, " why are you dawdling along in this fashion. I've watched that lazy light for the last fifteen minutes as you crawled down the hill, and I'm half dead with waiting for you. Where is the woman——"

8

He stopped and fell back with an oath as the light flashed up again and he saw my face.

" Who the deuce are you?" he stammered, " and what are you doing here?"

" I'm on the highway," said I, hotly, " and minding my own business."

" I'm not so sure of that," the man retorted, glancing at the lantern which I carried, " and unless I'm much mistaken you've got my lantern in your hand."

" I found it where the lady left it," said I. " If it's yours, you shall have it, but I'll have a look at you first,—and may be the coroner will thank me for it ; " and with that I held it up and let the rays fall on him.

He fell back livid, and I saw the face of an old man with white mustache and eyebrows. It was a fine military face, and one that I knew well in common with all the country for miles around. I was no less shocked at the disclosure than at the man's way of taking my action, for after an instant of silent rage, he launched out into a torrent of abuse the like of which I have never heard.

" And now," said he, when he had exhausted himself and his vocabulary, " give me my lantern. I've wasted both time and speech on you. Go your way, and see to it that you keep out of mine. I don't ask you why you are prowling here with my lantern, but I swear if I find you dogging me, I'll throw you into the sea."

He snatched his lantern and started up the hill.

"One moment," said I, and I planted myself with determination in his path. "My wit is too slow to keep pace with as fast a tongue as yours, but you have called me a thief, and that very plainly."

"And if I have," said he, but somewhat less aggressively, I thought, "you are lucky to have got off so easily. You can scarcely grumble at the terms if I am willing to ask no questions."

"Be damned for your terms and for your impudence," I answered, wrathfully. "You shall hear what I have to say before you stir out of your tracks."

He looked surprised, and I saw his disengaged hand dive into a pocket, but my blood was up and he might have emptied an arsenal into me without standing off the explanation I had started on. I told him how I chanced to be there and what had led to it, and his brow cleared as I went on.

"And now," said I, in conclusion, "I am ready for an apology."

He drew his hand from his pocket, and something came with it, and when his arm dropped to his side I saw the steel of a pistol glisten. But he was man enough to admit his error, and after his fashion he did it well.

"See here," he said. "You caught me at a disadvantage, and I lost my temper—damnably. It's a weakness I'm forever doing penance for, and I offer you a sincere apology. Now, I don't know you from Adam, and I don't know what you have seen or heard beyond what you choose to tell. I have blundered into an indiscretion with a stranger, and you are on the edge of a personal matter of my own, and something which is none of your business. I do not use the phrase offensively," he added hurriedly, "but God knows the mess is none of yours, and if I have been grossly imposed upon, I shall not mend the matter by taking you into my confidence. I mistook you for another man, as you were quick enough to see, and then I suspected yourself. I take your word and you must take mine. And let me remind you before we say quits, that it is a gentleman's part to hold his tongue and encourage forgetfulness sometimes. Why, man," he burst out impatiently, "you do not even know my name——"

"I beg your pardon, Colonel Forward," I

interrupted, with dry emphasis,—and he swore again under his breath as I spoke—"but I will make you no promise. I take your apology, for you are speaking like a man now, and you are dealing with one. I am no meddler, and I know enough of the double edge of gossip to give it a wide berth. I can say no more than that, and if you are a wise man you will be content."

"There are more ways than one to make a man forget," he said, coolly, with a significant movement of his arm, and then he thrust the pistol fiercely in his pocket, and held out his hand. "That was a cowardly speech," he said impulsively, "and as unworthy of me as the thought which prompted it. I am not a coward, but I am an old man and sorely put upon, and you must not misjudge me."

I had taken his hand, and as he spoke my pity went out to him.

"We will call the account settled," said I, "unless I can help you."

"No, no," he answered, brusquely, dropping my hand, and recovering his old manner. "Believe me, I have no use for you whatever. You would much better go straight home and take a sleeping-powder—and now let me bid you good-morning."

I was chagrined, but we saluted each other with elaborate civility, and I stood aside to let him pass. And as he went by with his head so stiff in the air, the pity I had volunteered died a sudden and violent death, and I vowed he was a bumptious old fool. When I reached my gate and looked behind me, the Colonel's lantern was half-way up the cliff, and from the bobbing and plunging of the light I knew that between the wind and the roughness of the road he was having a hard time to keep his way.

I OVERHEAR A COLLOQUY

THE net result of my interference that night had been a pointed snub from the biggest man in the county. I thought on this with considerable disgust, but I drew a sort of negative consolation from the fact that Colonel Forward had not recognized my face, or if he had, had made no sign.

My sleeping-room occupied the whole front part of my small house, on the second floor, and its windows gave upon the road and upon either side as well. As I was getting into bed, a gleam of light danced across my wall, and I looked out. The Colonel, homeward bound, was trudging past alone. There was dejection in his gait, and I was petty enough to rejoice at the thought that his errand had failed of its purpose—whatever that might have been. And with that thought I tried to go to sleep.

I had not yet succeeded when I was aroused by sounds in the road, and I stole out of bed and to the window. I could distinctly hear a man's voice high with anger, and the pleading tones of a woman pitched in a lower and conciliating key. They grew louder as I stood there, and soon I heard the sound of their shoes as the pair approached from the cliff; and so marked was the difference that I could almost see the swinging stride of the man and the half-run of his companion as she struggled to keep up with him. Then the wind brought me scraps of their talk, and I did not scruple to listen the more keenly for that.

"Before God," said the man, "I'll have no more of this if you don't do as I tell you. Haven't I banked everything on this—and all for you?"

The woman's quick retort had something of bitterness in it, and I saw why he had hesitated on his last words.

"All for me!" she said, and her gentle blood showed in her speech. "Oh, Richard, Richard, have I not sinned enough but you must set this against me? Heaven knows I have no thought or care that is not yours. Do you think it was nothing for me to turn on that old man——"

"Well, well," he interrupted, impatiently, "I know all that, but we have no time to talk

15

of it now. I know how bravely you have done for me against him, but we are still in the woods and there is more to do."

" I do not see——" she began, and I wondered how any man could resist the sweetness of her voice, when he broke in upon her roughly :

" Then thank God that one of us can see. Your foolishness has cost us heavily to-night. You shouldn't have been caught by the old man, to begin with, and you ought to have known better than run away with a lighted lantern. Of course he would follow the light."

I heard her sobbing quietly. They had halted in front of the house.

" Then," he added, his anger seeming to increase as he dwelt upon the subject, " as if that were not enough, you must begin waving the damned thing before I came up with you, when I had repeatedly told you that that signal meant we were not ready for the boats and would stay ashore !"

" Oh, Richard, don't," she cried. " I know what a blunderer I am, and how I hinder you, but I do the best I can."

" Molly, Molly," said he, gently, " I know that you're the dearest, truest little woman on earth, and I ought to be shot for wounding you."

I thought so, too. I did not know the merits of the thing, but I felt I could have fought for that woman, and my fingers itched for a twist at the man's collar. But he was clearly beside himself, for after that outburst of tenderness his anger got the better of him again.

" It was all so foolish, so foolish ! " he said. " Even that wasn't enough, but you must do the thing up brown, as a woman always does, so you put your light out and threw your lantern away, after first forgetting to have any matches about you. Who ever heard of a woman with a match ! "

He stopped and laughed loudly—but whether at his own humor or the woman's distress I do not know. She called to him in alarm.

" At least," she said, with some spirit, " I am not fool enough to shout the whole country on our track."

" You are right there, at any rate," he said, quickly checking himself, " and I am the fool. But if I'm to take your word, there isn't a house within hearing of this one, and if we've got to wake this man up we may as well do it by laughing at each other as by swearing at him."

" So," thought I, " you're after me," and

I reached out for my revolvers that lay ready on the dressing-table. I began to have qualms of conscience about the glass bottle and the pipe, but the woman quelled them the next moment.

"Is there no other way?" she said. "It is no great hardship to spend the rest of the night out there. It will be daylight anyway before you can get me aboard, and this man will be suspicious of us if we wake him up at this hour for a lantern and a match. What excuse can I make him?"

"Take your own way," the man said, bluntly, "and forgive me if I am harsh, but for God's sake go and have it done with."

While I wondered what to do, I heard her fumbling with the gate latch. They were still a minute and then she gave a little cry.

"Oh, Richard," she said, with such real distress in her voice that I was near calling out to her myself, " I have lost one of the bottles. There were three, and I have only two in my pocket."

He gave a great oath and started back the road they had come. She called to him to wait, but he seemed frenzied on his new errand and forgetful of the one that had brought them to my door, and ran swiftly on. I heard the girl crying softly there in the dark, and my tongue broke its bonds.

"Madam," said I, gently, "if you will let me help you——"

I might have gone on to offer her the bottle I had picked up, had not she interrupted me in her terror.

"No, no," she cried, hardly above a whisper, running close under the window in her eagerness as she spoke ; "no, not a word more. I do not know what you have heard——"

"I will not deny," I began ; but she burst in again.

"Do not tell me what you have heard," she begged, "and as you value your life and pity me, forget that you have heard anything."

"I would rather——" I began again, thinking of Colonel Forward, but she did not let me finish.

"Sir," said she, "you do not know me and I do not know you, but you are a man, and a kind one by your voice. Do a woman this one act of kindness. Forget all that you have heard, or persuade yourself that you have dreamed it and never tell the dream. Please God, you shall never see my face, and never again hear my voice. I on my side will forget that you have spoken to me. And that the confidence may be more to you, let me tell you that the sound of your kind voice has been blessed to me this night."

She was standing in the walk. and I could dimly see her form in the darkness, and her up-turned face.

" I will promise you," said I, more moved by her voice and manner than I had supposed it possible for me to be by any woman, " and may God help and pity you, whoever you may be."

I had hardly spoken when the man hallooed from the road beyond. She started in alarm.

" Good-by," she said, "and Heaven bless you ! " and she was gone.

I stood and listened to the quick patter of her feet as she left my door, and as the distance widened between us, that sound was merged in another that rose faintly from the sea and waxed as it came. The rain was falling and the storm had come.

When I awoke from my sleep later in the day, a hopeless northeaster was raging, and the rain was beating furiously through my open windows. As I put on my coat, a bulging pocket reminded me of the mysterious bottle, and I took it out and examined it. There was nothing peculiar or interesting about the thing, and I was disappointed at that after the fuss the man had made over its loss. It was a small bottle

with a glass stopper, as I have said, and about
half full of a coarse substance that looked like
sand. The pipe was even less interesting,
though it was a pretty piece of briar, and as
black as ebony from use. I carried them
downstairs with me and put them away on the
top shelf of a little cupboard of my library,
where I kept my pipes and tobacco.

But the ample leisure of a day indoors gave
me opportunities for speculating upon my adventure, which I could not well avoid. And
though I had not the slightest clue to go on, I
found myself building up the most elaborate
theories to account for the strange actions of
the three trespassers upon my solitude.

My own habits of life, as I have said before,
brought me few acquaintances,—those only to
whom I was driven by my necessities, and some
few whom chance had led to me. In neither
class was Colonel Forward. I knew him for
my next neighbor, living just over the hill
toward the village, and I had seen his picture
in the school histories, for he had achieved
some reputation in his chosen calling. He was
a haughty old gentleman, according to all ac-
counts, who since his retirement from the army
had lived almost as much of a solitary as myself, and for any likelihood of a casual acquaint-

ance between us he had as well lived in Guinea as on East Crag. That feature of his life and character had always interested me, and I had often wondered why, with wealth and influence at his command, he chose to isolate himself from all but the few retainers who made his grounds their home. I fancied that the death of his wife some years before had left this mark upon him.

Now that I thought the matter over, his manner at our meeting encouraged the idea that he and the strange pair whom he was pursuing when I came upon him, were confederates in one scheme. But on the other hand, the bearing of the man and woman, when they stopped under my window in the night, was open only to the construction that they were avoiding being seen in the neighborhood, and most of all by the Colonel himself. Up to that time the thought of connecting the stiff old soldier with crime or dishonorable intrigue would have been repugnant to me under any circumstances. But I suppose the sting of personal resentment had its weight, for when I thought of his railing words and his threatening attitude, I was filled with suspicion and distrust.

As to the woman, I cannot even now tell you what I thought of her or where my impressions lay. I somehow felt myself her sworn champion after our strange interview. I blindly pitied her, and hated those whom I thought her persecutors with a fervor that may have been ill-judged, but certainly had its rise in the better instincts of my nature, as our hates so often have.

But it was her companion around whom the greatest interest centred, after all. So far, he was to me only a big voice out of the dark. I tried to picture what such a man should look like, and I longed to see him.

In this idle fashion I let the forenoon pass, and I had taken up and dismissed the mysterious trio a hundred times, for a guess, when I turned in sheer weariness to my library window. A strange man in sailor rig was standing in the walk looking curiously toward my house. The sight of me at the window cured his indecision, and instead of retreating he turned boldly to the door. My instinct told me that here was the man I had been waiting for, and I knew that when he spoke I should hear the voice that had drawn me out of bed the night before. And at that a load fell from my mind, for I felt that so long as I could keep him by me, I might see her again. Indeed, I had not known up to that moment how long the day had been.

23

I ENTERTAIN A VISITOR

I HEARD him scrape the mud from his boots, but I had the door open before his hand had reached the knocker. He passed by me into the hall without a word, though I fancied he looked surprised at the genuineness of the welcome. When I had closed the door again, he opened his mouth.

" You are the master here ? " says he.

" I am," I promptly answered, taking my cue from the familiar voice. " You look cold and wet. Come in where it's warm."

" You're the right sort," said he, heartily, " and I will. I've been out on the rocks for ten hours, and I'm soaked to the marrow."

I had brought him into the library as I spoke, and pushed up a chair before the little fire that was burning on my hearth. He dropped into it with a sigh.

" Will you take it neat," I asked, touching a matter that I knew lay next his heart, " or shall I make it hot, with a little sugar ? "

He looked at me with open admiration.

" Raw," he murmured, and as I fetched a bottle and a glass, " Do they breed many of your sort here ? " he added, with a kind of roar. " God bless you for a man after my own heart ! You're the first I've met on this damned coast, and I want to shake hands."

He got on his feet as he spoke, and I saw what had escaped me before, that he was near done with exhaustion. He swayed unsteadily, and would have fallen if I had not supported him and dropped him gently back into his chair. Yet all this time I could have knifed him for dread of what he had done to the girl, for he had not been in the best of humor when she had run to meet him the night before.

" Never mind that now," I said, soothingly. "Take your drink and keep your thanks till you've got your nerve back."

I may have overdone the hospitality, for instead of answering me he looked up with a scowl.

" None of that," he growled, suspiciously. " What are you up to, anyway ? It strikes me you're just a little bit too good."

" From your manner, I am," said I, with a touch of temper, " and I shall be glad to see your back when I've made you a man again.

Just now I'm doing what I would do by any vagabond who fell in my way."

He sat up in his chair and looked me straight in the eyes, and I stared back at him without flinching. He was a powerfully built man, of perhaps forty-five, with a handsome face bronzed by exposure, a short light beard and mustache, and that certain mark of breeding that nothing can wholly erase. Just now his clean-chiselled features were a bit drawn, though even in his distress he looked every inch the sailor that he was. But his eyes were his strong point, and I have yet to see the pair that will match them for expression. They were blue or gray or green, fire, stone, or water, as the mood behind them changed, and I swear they were all these things in as many seconds as he looked at me. But they softened in an instant, and he held out his hand for the glass.

" You've a sharp tongue," said he, with a weak laugh, " but I guess you're about right, and here's my regards," and he gulped down whiskey enough to have made my head swim. Then, with a sigh that was half sob and half laugh, he fell back in his chair and closed his eyes.

I turned to the window and gave him a chance to pull himself together, which he was not slow to improve.

"I'm a new man," says he, presently, "or rather, I'm myself again after that whiskey of yours, and now I wish you'd overlook my rudeness. I'm not in the habit of walking uninvited into men's houses, and if you'll take my apology and believe how honestly I thank you for your kindness, I'll go."

He had got up as he spoke, and I was frightened for a moment lest I really lose him.

"You'll stay here as long as you please," said I, quickly, "and until you get back strength enough to fight your way out, you'll stay as long as I please."

He shot me an odd look at that, but he laughed good-naturedly as he pushed his chair closer to the fire and sat down again.

"Now," said I, seizing my opportunity, "I'm not only the master here, but I'm the cook and the house-keeper and the chambermaid. You can reach the whiskey, and I'll go out and get us a bit of dinner."

"I won't lie," said he, with a sigh. "I've eaten nothing but spray for nearly twenty-four hours."

All the time I was busying myself in the kitchen, I was planning openings for a conversation that should get me somewhere; yet for the life of me I could think of nothing satisfactory unless I plumped straight to the point, and that, I saw, was more likely than not to make matters worse than ever.

He was standing at the window with a lowering face when I went in to call him to dinner, but he brightened when he saw me, and he was the promptest guest at table that I have ever entertained.

It had been long since I wished to see a woman in my house, but the recollection of that girl's voice stuck to me, and I pictured her shivering on the rocks while this fellow ate his fill indoors. Perhaps there was a dash of sentiment in my reflections, for I was not so very old as years go, you must remember. Indeed, I thought it was nip and tuck between my guest and me on that score, though he probably had a little the advantage.

"There is more than enough for us both," I said, tentatively. "It is a pity we have no guest at hand."

"Had I known your hospitality last night," he said, with a laugh, "I might have helped you out. As it is, I have no hunger but my own to look out for to-day."

It was the man's tone of relief that set me at my ease, for I knew he had the woman in his mind, and I was sure he could not have spoken

28

so if she were in danger, or if he had dealt badly by her. I did a foolish thing.

"Here is her health," said I, and reached my glass out to clink his.

"What the devil do you mean?" said he, springing from his chair and glaring at me. "Whose health?"

I saw my error, and for once my wit was awake. "The hostess who should have presided here were I the lucky man I could wish to be," said I, coolly.

He dropped into his chair and lifted his glass to his lips.

"With all my heart," says he, eagerly, and drank deep. I held my tongue after that, and he ate his dinner with the coarse relish of a man half starved.

"This is the first time to-day," he began, as we arose from the table, "that I've had an appetite for smoke. You don't mind a pipe?"

And when I shook my head, he fished a jack-knife and a piece of plug tobacco from his pocket, and whittled off enough to fill a pipe. But when he came to the next stage I saw that something was wrong, for I had watched him with a purpose of my own.

He felt in each of his pockets by turn, and then nervously by twos, and finally in all of

them all at once, or so it seemed, as a man will
when he has reached the critical point of search
for something lost. So I asked him what was
amiss, though I very well knew.

" Why," said he, quite crestfallen, " I've
lost my pipe."

" Then you've fallen in with the right man,"
I said, "for I'm strong on pipes. Will you
have a clay or a briar or a meerschaum ? "

" You don't understand," he said, a little impatiently. " I've no great stock of sentiment,
but that pipe was an old friend. I've had it
Lord knows how long. I may have left it on
his table," he added, more to himself than to
me ; and then abruptly, " Do you know Colonel Forward, of East Crag ? "

" I have met him," I replied.

" And is he a friend of yours ? "

" No," said I, " and I distrust him."

But my thrust did not have the effect that I
had anticipated, for the sailor looked mightily
pleased at this reply.

" Good," said he, roundly. " I like you the
· better for that."

" But what has Colonel Forward to do with
the matter ? " I could not help asking.

" I have not said he had anything to do
with it," the man answered, sharply. " As for

the pipe, I dare say I've dropped it on the rocks, and I'll look for it later. Meanwhile, if you've an old briar you can spare, I'll trouble you for it."

I saw from his manner that he was not to be drawn out further, so I held my peace, and we lighted our pipes. The conversation lagged, and I left him for a little while. When I returned he had fallen asleep. I sat and watched him for an hour, and though he often stirred at the noise of the storm, he never once opened his eyes, and I was glad for him to get the rest that I saw he so sorely needed.

Suddenly, above the howl of the wind a gun boomed to the east. To a dweller on that coast there is no such ominous and dismal sound in a storm as this. It is like a fire-bell in the night, but a hundred times more doleful and significant. To the south of us and nearly a mile off shore, a wicked reef shows at low water, and cuts off that side of the cape from the approach of ships. There is a light on the reef, but in thick weather the coasters from the north sometimes lose their bearings and crash into the Crag, where the water is deep enough to float a war ship close in shore. My trained ear told me that the sound came from the east.

However soundly the sailor had slept, he was

on his feet as quickly as I, broad awake and quivering with excitement.

" Did you hear that," he cried, " or was I dreaming ? "

" It was no dream," said I, already running for my storm coat, and as I spoke I heard the sound again.

" They're off the Crag," I shouted back to him, but he had pulled his cap down firmly, and was turning up the collar of his coat.

" By God ! " said he, " then it's all right ! " And before I could join him he was tugging madly at the front door.

It seemed to me that it was all wrong, but I had no chance to tell him so, even if I had thought it worth my while. He was a better runner than I, and he had the start of me, besides which I had my weak ankle to favor, so that when I got into the road, he was a hundred yards away, running like a deer toward the Crag.

I followed him as well as I could, but he kept his lead, and when I reached the cliff he was pacing back and forth upon the very verge of it and scanning the sea, or as much of it as his eyes commanded, for the rain and spray made it impossible for us to see much farther than the breakers at our feet.

32

"Did you hear it again?" he roared into my ears as I came up. I shook my head.

"Two guns," he bawled. "Then it's all right, and there'll be merry hell before morning," and he shouted with laughter that I could fairly hear above the din of the storm.

I believed the man was mad, and fell back out of his way. No thought but of a stranded ship and a drowning crew had come to me at the sound of the guns, and the horror of it and of his shocking flippancy lay upon my face as I looked at him. He saw the look upon my face and the laugh died out of his.

"What's the matter with you, man?" he shouted, coming a step nearer.

"Stand off," I cried, backing down the hill. "Are you a fiend or a mad man, that you can make sport at a time like this?"

"Stuff," said he, in a changed voice. "I keep forgetting that you know nothing about all this. No, I'm neither mad nor a fiend. But I know a man at East Crag who'll be both before to-morrow morning, and I've beaten him this day. I swear, if you were a day younger and our acquaintance an hour older, I'd make you dance with me here on the turf. But come down out of the wind now, and I'll ease your old-maid mind."

33

And with that he seized me by the arm, and half dragged me down the hill. I thought he would have stopped when we reached the level, but he kept on without a word until we came to the house.

IV

IN WHICH A BOTTLE FIGURES

H E shook himself when we got inside again, and stalked furiously back and forth across the room for some minutes, apparently forgetful both of me and of his promise. I watched him from a corner and at length he took his old seat before the fire.

"And you think I'm crazy, eh, old lady?" says he, turning toward me. "Well, may be, may be, but whether or no, it's fitter that we should know what to call each other, and my name is, let us say—Nicholson."

"That is as it may be," I answered, a bit piqued at the name he had given me and the obvious concealment of his own. "I am John Hunt—to you and to everybody else."

"So much by way of introduction," he said, ignoring my sneer. "And now, Mister Hunt, you may set your mind easy about that ship. I know her well,—and her cunning skipper,"—I thought the man balked at the word, and a shadow crossed his face; but he went on,—"I know what the two guns mean, and it isn't danger. There's no wreck, and no drowning crew, and no misery aboard her, you can wager. The misery's all ashore," he added, and here again there was the faintest touch of bitterness in his voice; but he smiled grimly and gave me a patronizing look that prompted me to pull him down a bit.

"I'm glad to hear it," said I, still nettled; "and suppose now you tell me what became of the young lady."

If ever a man was disconcerted it was he. He started clean out of his chair with an oath, and then asked me, with a fine assumption of indifference, what the deuce I meant. I saw I was in for it at last, and told him as much as I chose, with such reservations as my caution and my promise to the lady suggested—and among these I made no reference to the glass-stoppered bottle.

He seemed a good deal put out at my knowledge of the matter, but he carried it off very well, and when I came to relate my meeting with Colonel Forward, he pursed his lips and whistled. From that point his embarrassment was lost in his newly aroused interest. When I had finished, I gave him his pipe, which he took rather sheepishly, I thought.

" So it was you," he said, with a bad look in his eyes, " who alarmed us last night and got our lantern. Well, well, let it go," and he laughed, uneasily.

" I wish I had known it was you, and not the old man pawing around on the cliff there," he said again, after a little pause ; but from his manner I was truly glad he had not been undeceived. Then he added, with a manifest effort to keep pleasant :

" Well, so much the better. You shall both make it up to me, depend upon that."

He scowled at the fire a moment, and then the wrinkle left his forehead and he chuckled.

" And all the time I was thinking myself so damned smart," said he, " you had this in you. That toast, now——"

" To be quite frank," I interrupted, " it was to the lady of the lantern."

" Umph," said he, swallowing hard as though my phrase disagreed with him. " Well, Mister John Hunt, you may quiet your fears if they lie in that quarter. She's a dear girl, is Molly, and she's not likely to suffer through me."

37

He was eying me queerly as he spoke, and perhaps I looked sceptical, for he frowned suddenly, and got on his feet with an oath that I need not repeat.

"See here," said he, swaggering before me in an attitude that I liked no more than the challenge in his wicked eyes. "Look me in the face—straight in the eyes, now. My name is Nicholson. Do you hear, Mister Hunt? *Nicholson !*"

He waited, and I thought his eyes shifted a bit as I looked him full in the face. Yet he looked for all the world as though he would like nothing better than for me to give him the lie then and there; but I frankly did not know the man, and such doubts as I had I did not scruple to put behind me. Under the circumstances, I would have called him Saint Peter, had he so much as suggested it, and never asked him for credentials. Indeed, my eagerness to take him at his own valuation must have been apparent, for he turned away with an impatient laugh as he stopped speaking.

"There, there," said he, "I'm upset, and that's a fact. Damn it, man, why couldn't you have minded your own business and let the girl go without following her;" and then, as if he had said too much, "about those Forwards," he added, hastily. "Do you know the family?"

I shook my head, but he looked incredulous.

"How long have you lived here?" said he.

"Twenty years," I answered.

"What!" says he, sharply, "you have lived here longer than Colonel Forward himself"—he looked suspiciously down at me again—"and you mean to tell me that you don't know your next neighbor, and more or less of his business? No, no, no, man. That won't do, you're a contradiction in terms."

It was one way of calling me a liar, and not a very polite way at that. I felt my cheeks flaming as I stood up and faced him.

"You've gone too far," said I, "and I'll submit to your bullying no longer. You and your Forwards are one to me, and I'm heartily sick of the sight of you. By the help of God and the absence of womankind, I've been away from gossip half my life, and if a silly woman with a lantern——"

He stopped me with a quick gesture.

"You forget yourself," said he, with a dignity that confused me. "Confine your abuse to me."

The rebuke brought me down.

39

"You're right," said I, cooling in an instant, "and I thank you for reminding me; but I've no abuse for anyone."

"I am heartily glad," he replied, with no trace of irony.

"But," I went on, "I say once for all that I do not know the Forward brood. I never spoke to the old man before last night, and I want never to speak to him again. I only ask that God keep me shut of him and his, and you may all go hang for any interference from me. I've no stomach for meddling further with you."

He bowed, gravely.

"Have you quite done?" he asked, politely.

"No," said I, with a silly inspiration to do something smart, and I stalked across the room and whipped open the door of my little cupboard. "There's this besides. I've something here that belongs to you, and you'd better take it now."

I took the glass-stoppered bottle from the shelf, and wheeled around to him again. He had been watching me with a half-interested look, but the change that came over his face when he saw the bottle swinging in my hand was wonderful to see.

"Stop, you reckless fool," he shouted. "Put it down—put it down carefully—*carefully!* Good God, man, you handle it as if it were sawdust. Put it down, I say!"

Instead of approaching me, he was backing away with a celerity that would have been amusing had his terror not been so shockingly manifest. His face was the color of the stuff in the bottle, and I looked at him in dismay. Something of his alarm communicated itself to me, and when he saw me place the bottle cautiously on the table as he had ordered, the blood came into his face again and he drew a long breath.

"Put it back in the cupboard," said he, with more coolness. "Put it back and let it stay there, and mind how you handle it;" and as I gingerly replaced it on the shelf and closed the door, "Now," said he, "you may tell me where you got that bottle, if you please, and why the devil I've not known of this sooner."

We had changed places again. His anger was rising, and mine had lost itself in the shock of his surprising behavior. So I told him how I had found the bottle, and for having kept it from him, I made such excuses as I could. For a moment he did not speak, but stood as if deliberating whether to let it pass or to knock me down. Then his rage left him and I saw he was for peace.

"You gave me a start," says he, nervously, "but we'll call it square, since no harm's done. And now I caution you to let that stuff alone. It is mine, as you suspected, but it's safer in that closet of yours than in my pocket. Leave it there until I ask you for it. I swear," he added, drawing a deep breath of relief, "I thought for a minute you were for throwing it in the fire."

"And if I had," said I, "what then?"

He stared at me blankly, and opened his mouth to speak, but thought better of it and began humming an old hymn.

"Are you a Christian?" he asked, breaking off as suddenly as he had begun, and cocking his head on one side as he spoke. And when I looked puzzled, he broke into loud laughter and dropped back into the chair he had left.

"Well, well," he said, "we won't go into that. Perhaps your future's not secure, and theology isn't my strong point. But I owe you a word about myself——"

"And the young lady," I interrupted.

"Upon my soul," he said, with a frown, "you're bold enough about some things, Mister Hunt. Let me assure you that the young lady, my—my—niece, is quite safe, quite safe, or I'd not be loafing here. She's out of reach, thank God. And if you'll take my advice, you'll let that information suffice you until I choose to speak of her again.''

There was a strange mixture of sincerity and hesitation about this speech, and while I did not doubt that the woman had been sent aboard the ship, I had my own views about her being this man's niece. Each time she had addressed him during that brief dialogue before my house, she had called him Richard. But I had made no mention of that little excursion of theirs—remembering my promise to her. I did not answer him, and he watched me curiously as though he half suspected me of keeping something back.

"First of all," he said, after a pause, "do you suppose that anyone but the Colonel and yourself saw us last night?"

"No," said I, "and I will stake all I have that I am right. There is no lonelier bit of road on the coast than this, and since the fishing people abandoned their old look-out on the Crag, there has been no travel worth mentioning this side of Forward House."

"Excellent," he said, rubbing his hands together, and resuming his good humor suddenly as if a pleasant thought had struck him. "I envy you your place here," he continued with a sigh, and looked at me narrowly. I did not see the bearing of his remark, and as I made no reply to it, he came out boldly.

"Mister Hunt," says he, "I'm a hard-pressed man, and I want some help. You've been good to me so far, but I've more to ask." He sat up in his chair and leaned toward me. "There's a wrong being done—and you have already shown your sympathy for the poor girl who is to suffer by it," and he paused as if to note the effect of that speech upon me. "This is what I have to ask," he added, quickly, "that you will let me sleep under your roof to-night."

I have always lent myself readily to imposition, and there was a zest about this affair that tickled my fancy and stirred my blood.

"Stay and welcome," said I, "but I'll make you no pledges. Whatever I can do——"

"You'll do for the girl," he said, with a laugh I didn't like. And before I could remonstrate or finish the speech he had taken out of my mouth, he went on, "Thank you, Mister Hunt. You have a chivalrous soul."

44

I blush to think how ready I was to entertain him, but it does me good to remember that, however mistakenly I acted, I believed that I was serving her.

V

I YIELD A POINT

OF the yarn which Nicholson finally spun me that afternoon as we sat drying by my fire, I have now no adequate remembrance. In the main it was a smooth and creditable performance, but it has no place in the story I am telling, and for two reasons : It purported to be the man's history, which is no affair of mine, and it was chiefly a lie. I am tempted to transcribe it as a tribute to his ingenuity, for its skilful blending of truth and untruth to serve a temporary emergency, reveals to my mind the hand of a master.

The remarkable part of it was that he said as little as possible about his business on East Crag and the actors in the performance of the night before. So when he paused near the end of his tale to refill his pipe, I could not conceal my disappointment and my impatience.

" I am greatly entertained," said I, politely, " but you were to tell me something of the young lady and the old man from Forward House.''

'' Was I ?'' says he, apparently in honest surprise. '' Well, I'll say this much of Colonel Forward—he's a misguided man, Mister Hunt, to say no worse of him. In my cooler moments I acquit him of the greater blame, and believe him a tool in the hands of scoundrels,'' and he went on filling his pipe.

I gave him a chance to say more, but when I saw he had no disposition to do so, I spoke again.

'' And on that vague speech,'' said I, '' you rely on my help against him in an affair where all the presumptions are against you. It won't do, Mister Nicholson—if that be your name— I must know more, or——''

'' Or ?'' he repeated quietly, as I hesitated.

'' Or I wash my hands of the business,'' said I.

'' That seems a simple operation,'' he answered, '' but how do you purpose to do it ? No, no. You'll do no such thing, Mister Hunt. Believe me, you'll go further yet, and under no compulsion, either.''

He was looking quite calmly at me, and as he saw me about to speak, he raised his hand with a slight gesture of remonstrance.

"Wait," says he. "Do you know what I've saved that girl from? Well, they've kept her prisoner in that old barrack against her will, and they would have forced her to marry a bigger villain than the old man, if I hadn't interfered. For her I have risked and suffered much, and now I've saved her, and what further reckoning I have at that house shall be done to-night."

But I was not listening. I had no ears for anything after that speech about the marriage.

"Force her to a marriage?" said I, angrily. "Why, man, what business——" and there I stopped myself and reddened, for I saw him smiling at my wrath.

"Who is he?" said I, swallowing my anger.

"Have you heard of the old man's sailor son?" he asked after a pause, and he did not turn his face my way.

"No," I answered.

"Well," said he, quietly, "I've said enough."

"The damned villain," said I, and the man turned toward me again with a stranger look on his face than I had yet seen rest there.

"Yes, all of that," says he, with a smile; "all that, Mister Hunt, and more besides. I

48

know him well, and I speak from the heart when I say his sins appall me."

He leaned toward the fire and knocked the ashes from his pipe on the hearth, and something in his face, as the light shone on it, checked the question that was on my tongue.

"Hunt," said he, suddenly, jumping from his chair, "God bless your clever old heart! You're a good fellow, and I'll not do it, I'll not do it."

He was greatly agitated, and I stared stupidly at him as he approached me. He seized one of my hands in both his own and looked in my face, and his was white as snow.

How slight a thing sometimes makes or mars a noble purpose! At that instant, I knew the man's better instincts were on top, but the puzzled look in my face drew his attention, and as he looked, he laughed. And there was the turning point, for under that laughter his resolution melted. He flung my hand from him and walked to the window. And he stood there looking out on the road and drumming on the casement with his fingers.

"Mister Hunt," says he, without changing his position, "I'm calling on Colonel Forward to-night."

I made no answer.

49

"And I want a witness," he went on presently, and still I did not reply, for I knew what he was coming to.

"You are my reliance," he said again, slowly, "and I think he would hear reason from a neighbor, where he would have only curses for me."

Mindful of my own experience with the old gentleman, I had views on this point, but as I raised my head to reply, the white door of the cupboard stared back at me and I thought of the bottle inside. A dreadful suspicion flashed across my mind, and while I was still battling it, the man spoke again.

"It is for the girl's sake," he said, still drumming with his fingers, and I shivered as I fitted his answer to my unspoken thought.

"No," said I, with an oath, "I'll have no more to do with it. I'll tell you what it is— it's murder, and you'll hatch no schemes here."

He sprang away from the window and faced me.

"What!" he shouted, and came upon me bristling with rage. "What do you mean?"

"I mean the poison in that bottle," said I, standing up to him; and at that his wrath collapsed again, and he stepped back and surveyed me with a look of pity.

"Heavens!" said he, with evident relief. "What a detective you would make, Mister Hunt! Poison!" and he laughed. "And I suppose you think I'm planning to cram that stuff down the old man's throat, and that I want you along to see me do it! God bless my soul, how funny you are!"

"What is it, then?" I said, doggedly, and paid no heed to his sarcasm.

"The stuff in the bottle? A tonic, man," he said, dryly. "Good for the nerves. But see that you let it alone, and I'll take my oath it shall never be nearer Colonel Forward than it is this minute."

"That's all very well," I persisted, "but you are keeping something back from me——"

"How in the world did you divine it?" he interrupted, with mock seriousness.

"Will you tell me what that bottle is, and how you came by it?" said I.

"No, Mister Hunt," he answered, promptly, "I won't; but I'll tell you that it shall cut no figure to-night. Will that do you?"

"Since I'm not going with you," said I, "it's the same to me whether it cuts a figure or not."

I had reckoned on bringing him to terms, and I was chagrined at his reply.

"You shall do as you please," says he, care-
lessly. "I've said all I can, and if you don't
choose to help us further, at least I must not be
ungrateful for what you've done already."

He held out his hand, and as I took it,
"Good-by," he said. "I thank you, Mister
Hunt, and—do you watch that bottle until I
call for it."

And when I found speech to answer him, he
had passed out, and the front door was slamming behind him.

I think he had some confidence that I would
follow him, for he loitered in the yard as if
loath to go, in spite of his zeal to leave my
house. But at the first I was glad to be rid of
him, and I watched him with satisfaction from
my window as he finally turned into the road
and strode away toward Forward House. But
when he disappeared from view, I felt that
with him had gone great possibilities. Until
then I had kept my adventure well in hand,
but here was a most inglorious ending of what
had promised much. I dwelt again on what
he had told me and on the woman's plight,
and my heart misgave me. I wished I had
temporized with him. And that mood shaded
off into a burning curiosity to know more than
I already knew. I longed to look once more

upon that bottle, and dared not take it from the shelf.

He had been gone not upward of fifteen minutes, before I was straining my eyes for some sign of him returning, and when the time had stretched to half an hour, I was waiting on the door-step. A little later, alas, I had put on my hat and was walking in the road !

It had grown dusk, and I could barely see the top of the hill beyond. I glued my eyes to that point and waited hoping, and finally, to my great delight, an indistinct something moved in the road and gained outline as it approached. I knew the man's strong walk, and presently Nicholson had come up to me. He did not speak, but stopped beside me and peered in my face. Perhaps he was reassured by what he saw ; but his voice when he addressed me was full of dejection, and he had the manner of one suffering from keen disappointment.

"I am repulsed," said he. "It's no use, Mister Hunt, he will not see me alone."

" Have you been there, then ? " I asked.

" And where have you been ? " he questioned by way of answer and looking sharply at me the while.

" No farther than you see me now," I said, and the sharp look left his face.

"Yes," says he, with a sigh, dropping his eyes, "I've been there, and it was a fruitless errand. I am one man against the hosts of hell."

His bitterness grew on him as he spoke.

"Come in," said I, seizing his arm. "Come in and take a drink. You need it."

He came, as a matter of course, and when we had got inside the house again, dropped moodily into his chair.

"I can get no speech with him," he began, presently, "and I must give it up;" and he buried his face in his hands.

His bowed figure was inexpressibly sad to me in the firelight, and the man's manner touched me.

"Come, come," said I. "I hope it's not so bad as that."

"There's the one thing yet," said he, quietly, without lifting his head.

"And that?"

"I told him through his bolted door, of you," said he, "and he says he knows you for an honorable man, and respects you. If you will go there with me——"

He stopped and lifted his face from his hands.

"Did he say that?" I asked.

"More," Nicholson answered; "but I'll

not spoil you with it. It's plain you stand well hereabouts."

I have this to urge on my own behalf. I was a lonely man, far from the world that lay about me, and the honey of flattery was new to me. I drew him out, eager for whatever he chose to tell me of the old man's compliments, and they seemed most reasonable and fair. And he simulated a reluctance to tell me that only added to the charm. What chance had I against this schemer? It is sickening to me now as I think of it, and I wonder that I believed him, but I know many a wiser man than I whose rule is based on no broader principle than to believe what is pleasant to his ears, and reject the rest.

"You see how it is," said he at length, "and I can say no more."

"I will go with you," said I, blindly, "and do my part."

"Thank you, Mister Hunt," he answered; "for my own sake, and most of all, for Molly's."

We sat a little while without speaking. The day had quite gone out, and perhaps it was just as well so, for in a better light he had certainly seen satisfied vanity in my face, and I a more hateful look than that in his.

VI

I MADE shift presently to get a few lights in the house, and we foraged for something to eat, for Nicholson had taken his stand against my cooking again for him that day, and we compromised on cold meat and bread.

The wind had gone down with the sun, and the moon shone through the breaking clouds. Nicholson's spirits seemed to clear with the weather. He was constantly running to the window and pressing his face against the pane to get a view of the sky, whistling and humming to himself the while.

"At eleven," said he, "we will start for Forward House, and when I have settled with the old gentleman we will come back and I'll make you a punch."

It would be difficult to say what thought was uppermost in my mind. I felt I was a fool, and in for a bad business, and I resented the man's air of proprietorship. Deep down in my

56

heart I felt I should yet suffer for taking cause with him, but the woman's voice was in my ears. It was the cry of one in distress, and silenced my discretion. For my life I could think of nothing better at the moment than to demur at the lateness of the start.

"I am the general," he answered, "leave the campaign to me."

"But don't you think it would be as well to discount defeat?" I suggested. "Suppose the old man should stand us off—we are but two, against—how many?"

"Ah, Mister Hunt," says he, with a twinkle in his eye, "you don't yet know me. I have a way about me, and your whole theory of life is askew if you have still to learn that persuasion is the most effective form of coercion."

He chuckled, and I fell to wondering what his game was. One thing tormented me and I could not make it fit with any natural theory of his bearing to the matter. When Colonel Forward had accosted me last night, he had plainly mistaken me for this fellow, and though he had spoken with impatience, he had approached me as an ally, and not as an enemy. Yet Nicholson would clearly have me believe that things were far otherwise between them, and I knew that his call at Forward House was

57

to have no friendly errand as its purpose. But he led me off into conversation about things that had no bearing on his business, and I gave over thinking about it.

He was of the gayest all that evening, and I fell in with his humor. We drank and smoked, and he sparkled with a wit that charmed me and would have won me over to a more doubtful cause.

About ten o'clock, and as we still sat talking, I heard a faint noise outside, and far toward the sea, which sounded like a bit of song. Nicholson's face darkened in an instant.

" Did you hear that?" I asked, for I had seen him start.

" It was nothing," said he, but he scowled and jumped to his feet. " Do you sit here and I'll run out and have another look at the sky."

As the door closed upon him, I heard the sound again and more distinctly. It was a sea song, pitched by a man's voice. But it stopped abruptly a moment later, breaking short off in the middle of the tune, and I heard it no more. When Nicholson came back he seemed in better spirits than ever.

" Ho, ho, Mister Hunt," he shouted, with a laugh. " I thought there was no travel on your road by night. You fellows never know what's afoot.   I've just been talking with a boozy fisherman who was passing when I went out.   Your ears are stout, though, for it was he you heard singing.''

I thought he would have been annoyed, but he seemed rather amused at the encounter, and he burst out laughing at intervals after that, and when I asked him why, he would but laugh the louder and say :

'' That fisherman's song has tickled me.''

And finally he sang the song himself, in a big round voice that filled the house.   Then he improvised a verse lampooning the old Colonel, and sang it to the same air, which set me laughing.

'' You've missed your calling,'' said I. '' With such a knack at rhymes and all the Bohemian qualifications, you should live in print.''

'' No, Mister Hunt,'' says he, with mock seriousness, '' I aspire to be a hero of song rather than a writer of it.   Besides, we Bohemians have lost the trick of mountain climbing.''

He saw that I did not follow him.

'' Bohemia,'' he explained, gravely, '' lies in the shadow of Parnassus.''

But though he could give himself up to this sort of thing as heartily as any man I have ever met, I soon found he had his sterner side as well, for he was out of his chair before the last stroke of the clock for eleven, and there was a smart ring of decision in his voice when he told me it was time to go.

"Are you armed?" he asked.

"My pistols are upstairs," I answered, and I turned to go for them.

"No," he said, calling me back. "Leave them. There is no fool like a badly managed pistol."

I flushed at the insinuation, but he called me down with a look.

"Dear, dear," said he, wearily, "what a fellow you are for taking offence. I didn't mean anything. Take your damned pop-gun if you want to, but if there's violence ahead, I serve notice on you now that I'm well out of it."

After that speech there was nothing but to leave my pistols behind, and I did so. We were quickly under way and walking briskly along the road to the village. Ten minutes of that sharp pace brought us over the brow of the hill and to the gate of the Colonel's grounds, which lay just beyond.

Forward House stood well back from the road, on the south side, and the grounds were full of trees. A winding drive approached the house, which was of colonial date and style, with a broad veranda across the front and east sides. When we reached the gate, Nicholson stopped and put a finger on his lips.

"It's as well to be cautious," said he, in a whisper, "and since the old man has a bad temper and no wish to see me after last night, I'll ask you to go alone."

I looked at him in some surprise.

"Last night? I don't understand," said I, slowly. "You've been here to-day, and he's agreed to see you if I come with you?"

He nodded hurriedly in a flustered sort of way, and would not look me in the face.

"Well, then," I continued, "I'm not pining for an interview, Mister Nicholson. I've come here only to keep you in countenance——"

"Tut," he broke in. "You want the earth, Mister Hunt. Is there but one way to help me, and that by skulking at the rear? Would you show the white feather now? Come, do as I tell you and we shall see what comes of it."

There was a fine evasiveness about this, but the man had read me like a book—and his speech lodged where he meant it should.

"I beg your pardon," I answered, stiffening under his sneer. "I have promised to stand by you, and I'm not given to drawing back."

"Good," said he, cheerfully. "But you are too sensitive by half. I meant no slur upon your spirit ;" and without giving me a chance for further remonstrance, he went on with his instructions. "Go on to the front door and ask for Colonel Forward. If he will not see you, raise your voice and I will join you if we can do no better. But tell him you are alone, for if he should see me in his doorway or hear my voice, I have every reason to believe that he would shoot us both. Now go !"

And he fairly pushed me up the walk. But I rebelled again.

"You have brought me here unarmed," said I, holding back, "and here you are talking of shooting as though it were a part of your programme. Now I draw the line——"

"Let me save you the trouble," said he, contemptuously, "I'll draw the line and you may run back home. You're no use to either me or Molly. Shooting !" he sniffed. "As if you couldn't see with half an eye that I was joking. But my humor is always taken seriously."

Three minutes later I would have given considerably more than my means afforded, had I but taken him at his word and run home. But the man's ridicule was too much for me, and I did what many a good man had done before me, and let my pride make a fool of me. I even forgot to ask what I was to say to Colonel Forward, should I be lucky enough to get audience with the old man, and turned toward the house conscious only that Nicholson's eyes were on me. No light was visible about the place, and at first sight it might have been tenantless for any sign of life that showed. But as I looked again I thought there was method in the darkness, for the windows were barred and shuttered, and through the chinks I saw a faint light from within.

My observations were suddenly suspended, however, for before I had gone a dozen paces I heard hurried whisperings from the darkness about me, and as I reached the door and stopped, the road seemed suddenly alive with men who closed upon me from all sides and fell in on either flank in the shadows at my back.

So far my silly pride had brought me, but it left me at the door, and I would have run if I could. The truth which had half flashed upon me at Nicholson's speech when we entered the grounds, was clear as day. I saw myself the man's cat's-paw and started from the door, but twenty guns were bristling in my face, and the voice of Nicholson came to me out of the night.

"Steady, Mister Hunt," said he, quietly. "No turning back! Go on and follow your instructions! If you fail me now, there'll be shooting on this side the door."

And somehow his cool threat steadied my nerve, and I turned back without a word and pulled the bell.

I was bewildered, I grant you, by the man's sudden change of front, but I had sense enough to see the folly of resistance, and sense enough besides, even in that moment, to curse the day I had opened my door to the infernal pirate who had got the best of me.

After an agony of waiting on my part, some-one came into the hall from the far end of the house, and shuffled forward bearing a light. The steps came on and stopped just inside the door.

"Who is there?" called the man in the hall, and I recognized the gruff tones of the Colonel.

"Is that Colonel Forward?" I shouted, by way of reply.

"Who is there?" he asked again, with dis-agreeable emphasis, and paying no attention to my question.

My ancestors were Scotch and caution is

written between the lines of my family history.
I hesitated.

"Tell him," whispered Nicholson from behind. "Tell him, you damned puppet!" and
I felt something pricking my leg.

"John Hunt," I shouted, hastily.

"And who is John Hunt?" the Colonel
asked, in the same level voice.

"A friend and neighbor," said I, desperately. "The man who gave you your lantern
last night," I added, with a touch of diplomacy.

And that did the business, for the old man
evidently remembered my voice. I heard him
calling softly to someone inside, and more footfalls sounded in the hall. There was a parley
in whispers while I stood there in torture between the devil and the deep sea, and alas, I
did not know on which side of the door the
devil was! And then presently the Colonel
called out, "Wait a minute," and I felt rather
than heard each man of those behind me draw
a long breath.

The door was cautiously unfastened, and I
heard the bolts rasp as they were shot back,
and to my tense nerves there seemed a hundred
of them at the very least. Then in a flash the
light from within poured into my eyes and
blinded me, and the next minute is a blank.

The door had scarce swung open before the hall was filled with men cursing and struggling, and above all I heard the voices of Nicholson and Colonel Forward. The lamp had been struck from the old man's hand at the first rush, and we were squirming and jostling in the dark. And this, I am sure, saved life, for no man dared fire or use his knife lest he fall upon a friend.

VII

A FIGHT IN THE DARK

BEING in the van of the besiegers, I bore the first savage brunt of the attack, and had the wind well-nigh knocked out of me before I fairly knew where I was. I heard Nicholson's curses at my elbow, and then I got a smart blow in the face that roused the fight in me and drove my neutrality into retirement for the time.

In the instant that the light remained after the door opened, I had seen our opponents, and that picture of them remained stamped on my mind in the darkness. The fellow just facing me had attracted my attention by his youth, his great size, and the incompleteness of his dress, for though apparently ready for the fight, he had on only his shirt and trousers, and as I was shot forward against him, my shoe fell on his bare instep. This accident served me a good turn, for we had been struggling but a moment when someone had me in a powerful grasp and I felt a hand stealing swiftly over the breast of my coat, as if to determine to a certainty whether I were friend or foe, and there was decision in the clutch with which it sought and held my throat a moment after. My own hands went out instinctively, and I felt the flannel shirt of the man who had opposed my entrance. His other hand was at his belt, and as I reached it, it closed upon the hilt of a knife. But the man's grasp at my throat never relaxed, and I held his other wrist with a grip of despair.

" Let go," he cried, with his face close to mine, " or I'll strangle you where you stand. You should have kept away from here once you got away, for I swear you'll not have the chance this time unless you choose to give up the girl."

And then, by a sudden thought, I reached out with my right leg and began digging with my heavy shoe where I hoped his feet would be. He gripped the harder, but the tactics demoralized him, and when I got in one with my sharp heel on his foot he howled with pain, and so I kept him dancing and cursing till, in a lull, his oaths rang out so loud above the skirmish that one of the sailor men behind me shouted,

" Put a knife into that yelping cur ! "

And they took up the rush again with more energy than ever. But my assailant was game, and though I must have sadly bruised his feet by this time, he put his face close to mine and said :

" You may dance till you are tired, you damned scoundrel, but I know you, and you'll not get away from me. The old man shall have one less blight upon him before I'm done with you, and we'll settle that little affair of our own at the same time."

He had given up trying to get his knife out, and spanned my neck with both his hands as he spoke, and he would have made short work of me if assistance had not come unexpectedly. He had hardly finished speaking when some-one forced between us, and the man's wrists were wrenched off my throat, and I heard the blow that sent him reeling back against his next companion.

" You've made a slight mistake, my dear Henry," I heard Nicholson saying in an un-dertone. " Pinch my neck, if you like, or if you'll wait till this row is over, we'll have our little difference out like men." And then in a louder voice, " Is that you, Mister Hunt ? " he added, grasping at me. " On my honor

I'm sorry to have brought you into such a mess, but it will be soon over, and I trust you're none the worse for your shaking up.''

I had no chance to answer him, for he gave a sharp call of command, and I was lifted off my feet and carried bodily down the hall by the quick responsive rally of his men.

I saw a sliver of light ahead of me, and heard the tearing of woodwork, then the door at the inner end of the hall burst open with a crash and the light streamed out upon us. There was a fresh rally at this, and before old Forward's men could raise and use their guns, the sailors were down upon them and the battle was over.

It was a strange spectacle that I looked upon. The big bare hall was full of men in many stages of dishevelment, and save for the sound of their heavy breathing after their exertions, the place was suddenly silent. Crowded into one end of the hall and against the broken door that had shut off entrance to the room beyond, the house party stood at bay. There were five of them besides the Colonel himself, and of these, all but their leader and the big fellow who had so nearly done for me in the scrimmage were submissive as sheep when they saw Nicholson and his twenty men, armed and blinking in the light. But the fight was not dead in those two, and they stood glaring like tigers, though they saw the folly of resistance, and, like good soldiers, bided their time.

Facing them stood Nicholson at the head of his crowd, and though the victory was his, he had nothing to say for himself. It seemed to me that he dodged the Colonel's eye, and I thought it strange after all that had passed that night. Indeed, ridiculous as it may sound, he seemed at a loss to know what next to do.

For me, I cut but a sorry figure, and resented my position. I held aloof from them all, bitterly reflecting on the fool's part I had played. Yet the quick succession of surprising incidents had somewhat stupefied me, and I felt rather like wondering what would come next, than reviewing the experience I had been through.

I felt myself the conspicuous object in all that room, and perhaps it struck Nicholson in the same way, for it was to me that he first broke that singular silence.

"You look rumpled, Mister Hunt," said he in a voice that sent the eyes of his men in my direction; "I swear you look as if you'd had the six upon you all at once. Take him into the library," he added to one of his men, and with a manner that showed his familiarity with the house; "and keep an eye on him."

I made no answer but followed the man's
lead, glad to be away from that crew on any
terms, and we had scarcely reached the library
when the Colonel found his tongue, and I shud-
dered at the result.   His rhetoric flowed in
forbidden channels, the depth of which I had
until then never dreamed.   And he was well
seconded by another, whose voice I recognized
as that of the man who had done his best to
choke me.   My conductor closed the door upon
it, and coolly produced a cigar which he lighted
as he scrutinized me.   But neither of us spoke
and the tumult outside continued.

Presently there was silence again and the
door opened.   Colonel Forward came into the
room, and close on his heels came Nicholson.
On the threshold the younger man stopped and
called back.

" I'm not forgetting you, Henry," he said,
"and I'll wait upon you shortly."   And the
bare-foot man shot back a foul defiance which
was cut short off by Nicholson's closing the
door.

" You may go," said he to the man who
had been my guard, " and don't return.   Stand
outside the door and keep everyone away from
here, and when Mister Hunt joins you, as he
will presently, keep him within reach."

The man left the room with a knowing look, the door closed softly, and I was left with the two men whom I had so longed to see together. Colonel Forward did not once look in my direction, and I stole a glance at Nicholson. To my great surprise, his coolness had deserted him. He seemed like a man without reliance, and as he looked at the Colonel, who stood there in dignified silence, his eyes sought the floor and he swallowed nervously. But he mastered himself with an effort and turned to me.

"Mister Hunt," says he, "I wished you to remain here long enough to quit you from blame in Colonel Forward's eyes. You were no party to this thing, as I gladly testify, and what you have done you were deceived into doing. I should hate to have you suffer for your part in to-night's work, for I declare you are innocent of any complicity with me. And now," he added, turning to the Colonel with more boldness, "I will talk with you alone."

Up to that time old Forward had not spoken, but if his spirit had been subdued before, it blazed hot at this, and I could but admire his retort, though I confess it puzzled me.

"Will you, indeed!" said he, and mad as he was, he was the cooler man of the two.

" Now, I have my own views on that point, and
I'm damned if you will ! Whatever rights you
have as my son you have forfeited a thousand
times over, and I have no dealing with a liar
and a thief."

Nicholson turned purple, but he did not re-
sent the charge.

" Will you talk of all that before this man,
then ? " he asked, nervously, jerking his head
toward me, for I still stood there, not knowing
where to turn.

" Why not ? " said the Colonel, letting his
eyes rest upon me.   " I have met Mister Hunt
once before, and you yourself tell me that you
have duped him to-night. He will be the read-
ier for that to believe what I say. I see your
dilemma," he went on, with composure, " and
you have reckoned on my pride to keep me
from disclosing our relationship before him.
Well, I have no pride left, and you see your
mistake ; and now I say again in this man's
presence, you are my own son, but, God forgive me, you are as black a scoundrel as ever
walked ! "

" And there," says Nicholson, quite cool
again, " I'll not contradict you. I have no
time to pick phrases or make you pick yours.
Why should we quibble about it ? If my

offence outrages you, yours that forced me to this course is no less repulsive in my eyes. You know my desperate straits and my last resource. You know I see death and dishonor on every hand. Yet here you stand, full of years and honor, and with that at your hand which will put me on my feet again and take the halter from my neck—and you refuse me.''

The old man lifted his hand.

''You may sneer,'' Nicholson went on quickly, ''but I swear I am unselfish in what I do. For myself, it matters little when or how I go, and it's no great hardship to skulk about with a price on my head. But Molly has changed all that, and life is dear to me because of her——''

''You dare to speak to me of her!'' the Colonel broke in, furiously. ''You, a robber and a liar, and that girl——''

Nicholson's eyes looked murder, and he started forward with a quick gesture of remonstrance.

''Be careful,'' said he, ''and remember that this is a family matter. There's no room for a stranger in it, and I'll take Mister Hunt outside. I'm thinking he's heard too much as it is.''

''No,'' said the Colonel, peremptorily, ''he

shall not go. He has served your purpose, and now let him undo that mischief by serving mine. I want you now, Mister Hunt,'' he added to me, and like a flash of lightning and with an adroit movement that would have done credit to a man of half his years, he sprang upon Nicholson and pinned him against the wall.

No one could have foreseen so sudden an attack, and the sailor man was quite unprepared for it. And though he made some outcry and there was a noisy scuffle for an instant, the tramping and talking of the men around the house drowned it all. The library was a large room with windows running to the floor and giving on the west. These were open as befitted the season, but heavy shutters of solid wood took the place of outside blinds, and they were closed. Before I really knew what was going on, the Colonel had Nicholson by the throat with one hand, and had jammed him hard against the shutter of the nearest window, while with the other hand he drew the bolt that held the shutter closed. In another instant the two had fallen through five feet of darkness on the turf below. I followed cautiously and found the old man bending over the other, who lay unconscious and breathing heavily.

The Colonel groaned.

"Are you hurt?" I whispered.

"Hurt," he said fiercely, springing to his feet; "no, but he is."

Nicholson moved and half opened his eyes, and I brought my rude knowledge of surgery and medicine to account, and made such examination as I was able.

"He'll be all right in a jiffy," said I. "He's only stunned."

"Then there's no time to lose," the Colonel said, with a note of satisfaction in his voice. "We must get away before they miss us."

He seemed to take for granted that I would go with him rather than stay with the other, and for that slight mark of confidence I registered my thanks, and followed the old man swiftly across the lawn.

Our course led toward the thick woods that lay some distance away and behind the house, and was over a long stretch of open and irregular ground. His knowledge of the place helped him, of course, yet taking his age into account, the rapidity with which he got over the ground was amazing. I followed him as well as I might, and as often as I lost him, I called softly and he waited for me to come up with him.

We ran a half mile in this way, along the ridge of the hill, and away from the road, when the woods suddenly loomed up ahead like a blotch of ink on a dark carpet. Then the Colonel slackened his pace a bit, and we went on easily. When we had reached cover he wound in and out among the trees, in a sort of pattern, and with a dexterity that showed method, so that I was not surprised when he suddenly stopped in a dense piece of under-brush, and went plump on his knees and began pawing like a dog in the dead leaves.

VIII

I PASS A NIGHT IN THE WOODS

UP to this time no word had passed between us since we left Nicholson, and I watched the Colonel in silence as he dug there in the feeble light of the setting moon. Suddenly he stopped his work and turned to me.

"I am making so much noise," said he, "that they might come upon us and we never know it. Run out to the edge of the woods and stand guard. If you hear anyone coming, give an alarm—otherwise wait there till I call you back."

"See here," I answered, "I've had enough. Why in God's name should I be prowling about the country with either of you on a mission I know nothing of?"

"My dear sir," he said, with irritating politeness, "you really ask me too much. I know neither why you should take nor why you have taken, such an offensive interest in my affairs, but I accept the fact as it is, and

I'm planning for your good quite as much as for my own.''

"Then you may save yourself trouble," I replied. "If you want help from the village to beat those ruffians off and save your house, I'll go that far for you, but I'll not stay skulking here in the woods. Rather than that, I'm going home."

"You may go to the devil for anything I care," said he, coolly, "but it shall not lie on my conscience if your throat is cut before morning. I give you fair warning. These fellows think you have helped me to get away, and your belly will never hear from your palate again once they clap eyes on you to-night. As for the village, there's not a man there who'd lift a finger to save me from the cruelest death in the list, and if you go there with an appeal from me, they'll kick you out of doors, if they do no worse by you. You'd much better take pot-luck here."

Little as I knew of him, I knew there was truth in what he said, and I realized too that I must have aroused the wrath of Nicholson by my desertion of him. I had no hankering for an early meeting with any of that band, and I turned away and started through the brush.

"Well?" asked the Colonel.

"You may call if you want me," I answered. "I shall stay for the present."

"That's wise," said he, and began scratching in the leaves again.

But however plausible his reason for sending me away may seem, I knew it was a mere ruse of his to be rid of me for a time, and I kept asking myself as I went what lay buried there that I might not see. And though I had to fight my cursed curiosity, I went straight to the place of look-out without so much as once turning around. I could see lights twinkling at the house across the fields, and I fancied I heard the sound of voices in that direction. I made no question that our escape had been discovered, but though I waited at least fifteen minutes awake to every sound, I neither saw nor heard anything to indicate that we were followed. On the contrary, my first alarm came from behind me, where I heard the Colonel shouting my name with great oaths, and begging me for the sake of his Creator to come to him at once. I hurried back and found him grovelling on his stomach beside a shallow hole which he had scooped in the dirt.

"What is it?" I asked, breathlessly, bending over him. "Are you sick, man? What is wrong?"

"Can't you see what's wrong?" he wailed, clawing his long fingers into the dirt with fury. "It's gone, it's gone!"

"What is gone?" I asked, but he was muttering to himself and digging deeper into the ground with fresh zeal. After a moment he stopped again, and raising himself on his elbow, looked up into my face—and his own made a light in the dark, so white and haggard was it.

"Mister Hunt," said he, "I must go back to Forward House."

"What!" said I, aghast, "back into that gang of cut-throats!"

"This instant," said he, firmly. "Give me your hand."

I pulled him to his feet, and he stood a moment unsteadily.

"I won't ask you to risk your skin there," said he, "though you may give me a lift for a bit of the way if you'll be so good."

But I was spared expostulation, for nature interfered. He staggered as he spoke, and clapped a hand to each temple.

"Oh, oh, oh!" he moaned, and toppled over like a falling tree, into the hole he had made. I kneeled beside him and lifted his head to my knee. Then I loosened his collar and chafed his hands, and after a little he opened his eyes. But he only partially revived, and when I spoke to him he trembled as though he were afraid of me.

" Pull yourself together, man," I cried.

" No, no," he whined, " don't hurt me, don't hurt me ! It is gone, gone, gone ! "

And though I coaxed and threatened him by turn, I could get no more out of him than that, nor would he stir from his spot in the woods. I could not have moved him against his will, and there was nothing to do but lay him down and wait. I was sore tired, but I could not leave him so, and I did not dare to sleep, so I sat there and watched by his side the rest of the night. He cooled down as the hours passed, and finally slept, and at daylight I left him and went again to the open ground.

Smoke was curling from the chimneys of Forward House, and that was the only indication of life that my eyes first fell upon ; yet as I looked, doubtful whether to venture farther, I saw movement in the trees upon the Colonel's lawn and a moment later, two men emerged from the shadows and came with swinging gait across the fields toward me. I drew quickly back into the brush that skirted the woods at this point, and when I looked again, two more

men had come into view and the four were
headed for the woods. The leaders were well
in advance, and whatever hope I had entertained of the departure of the ship's crew, was
dissipated when I recognized Nicholson and
one of his men. I should have thought this
meant business for Colonel Forward and me,
if I had not known the second pair for the big
fellow who had engaged me in the hall, and
another man of the Colonel's own household.
Then I recalled the collision between Nicholson and the bare-foot man, and the former's
promise that their difference should be adjusted
after the manner of gentlemen ; and I was not
surprised that each of the principals carried a
light, thin fencing sword. I saw what was on
the cards and lay very still, while they came
on with business-like haste, the two in advance
keeping well ahead of the others and holding
no communication with them.

Just in front of the woods, and between me
and the approaching party, was a depression of
the earth that formed a sort of natural amphi-
theatre. The ground sloped on all sides to a
flat spot at the centre, perhaps twenty feet
square, and far enough below the level of the
surrounding ground to make a man standing
there invisible from Forward House and the

distant highway. The bushes behind which I lay concealed were not a hundred feet from this point, and at the very edge of the southern slope.

Nicholson and his companion came on without a word, straight down the slope to the grass plot at the bottom. There they stopped, and the leader stripped off his coat and waistcoat, and turned his shirt-sleeves back above his elbows. He carefully examined his sword, and tried the temper of the blade.

"Allison," he said slowly to his companion, "as long as I can remember, that sword and the one that Harry has, have hung together in my father's library. Harry and I have played soldier with them many a time, and when he got bigger, I taught him how to fence. I swear," he added, laughing softly, "I never thought they would serve us in such a pass as this!"

He stopped speaking as the second pair approached, and my quondam assailant stripped himself as Nicholson had done, their two friends standing idly by in apparent unconcern. I watched them breathlessly, all fear for my personal safety having vanished when I knew their errand.

They wasted no time, and were quickly facing each other, their swords drawn and their brows contracted. They were well matched in size, and I was struck by their strong likeness to each other in face and feature ; but Nicholson looked the elder by a good ten years. The man from Forward House took his position and lunged viciously out with his weapon.

"Stop!" shouted Nicholson, easily parrying the thrust, and each drew back. "Harry," he continued, in a voice that was new to me, "think what you are inviting and what this means. We are sons of one father, and as you yourself say, this thing is murder for one of us. Bad as I know myself to be, I stop far short of wishing that. You say I have wronged you, and perhaps I have—but not as you think. I am a rebel against my father, and your lot lies with him. So far I am your enemy. But as to Molly—I love her and she loves me, and there's an end of it. If it were otherwise, I would say no word, but she has chosen. Why can't you take it like a man ? Do you suppose I will give her up because a man she detests wants me to——"

"You damned hypocrite," the other cried, with sudden rage, "shut up your cant and come on ! If you're the better man, you have only to prove it."

"As you please," said Nicholson, with a flash of his ugly eyes. "Come on, you puppy! If you want it so much, by God, you shall have it!"

They were good swordsmen, both of them, and it was no stage play. But I noticed that Nicholson stayed more on the defensive, and spent his time parrying the wicked lunges of his adversary, who plainly fought for blood. They were breathing heavily after two minutes of such hot work. Again and again Harry drove his blade like lightning at the other's breast, and each time it shot aside on Nicholson's superb guard. But I saw a change come over Nicholson's face, and his lips tightened. His features hardened and a bad look lay in his eyes. Finally, as the other pressed him more fiercely, he caught the blade on his own, and with a supple motion of his wrist sent it twisting from Harry's hand. And as Harry stood disarmed and at his mercy, Nicholson burst out again.

"Don't tempt me further," he cried. "Stop while you can, and before it is too late for either of us."

But Harry had regained his sword.

"You should have used that opportunity," he panted. "It was a coward's chance. Come on!'' And he fell to again more fiercely than ever.

"Then take it, you fool," Nicholson cried, and changed his tactics.

He lunged forward, and Harry caught it on his blade and smiled. His coolness had come with his second wind, and Nicholson was just getting mad. Nicholson swore, and his arm shot out again, but Harry parried neatly and returned the thrust so cleverly as to scratch his antagonist's cheek, and the hot blood, eager for an outlet, ran down and spattered in big drops on his shirt. And that maddened Nicholson, and he did what no man should dare do unless he knows the limitations of the other's eye and arm, or longs for sudden death: he tried that wicked outside thrust that curves toward the heart, and for the flash of an eye, as his arm went out, his great heaving chest lay open. Quick as a cat the other was in upon him, and the blade shot into Nicholson's breast like a needle into silk, and when it came out the blood followed in a stream.

It was no scratch, but the man was not done for. He shivered and parried the next thrust that his antagonist was following it up with. But his judgment was gone, for again his arm went out for that outside thrust, and I groaned

for him, for again the lightning of the other's
eye and arm drove the blade home before
Nicholson's had fairly started on its journey.

"Damn you," gasped the wounded man.
"You're an apt pupil, Harry. And to think
I spent days myself teaching you that trick!"

He reeled and lunged forward again, but his
blade glanced weakly aside on Harry's waiting
guard and he fell on his face in the grass.

The seconds, friend and foe, were over him
in an instant, but his adversary stood aside and
looked on with apparent indifference. They
turned the fallen man over on his back, and
Allison ripped his shirt open and bound his
wounds with a hand that showed skill and
practice. Then he turned savagely on young
Forward.

"We will get him back to the house—your
man here and I—according to our arrange-
ment," said he. "I don't know how badly
off he is, and perhaps I can fetch him around.
As for you, you know the agreement, and I
trust you to go and hold your tongue. You're
under truce now, but God help you if you ever
fall in my way again, and damn you whether
or no for what you've done this morning."

Without waiting for a reply, he turned to
the third man, and together they lifted Nichol-

89

son tenderly from the ground and started slowly back to the house. And Harry Forward said not a word, but stood and watched them as they ascended the slope; then he followed slowly in their train. He still carried the sword he had used so effectively, but his grasp upon the hilt seemed mechanical, and I doubt if he knew the thing was in his hand. His eyes were fixed on the little party ahead, and in this way he wandered on behind for a hundred yards or more. Then, with a sudden start, he looked down at the dripping steel he carried. He stopped and held it out at arm's length, and stared at it as though he had but just realized what it was. The next instant he had sent it spinning through the air, and abruptly changing his course, he strode quickly off to the west and disappeared in the woods behind his father's house.

IX

THE VILLAINS DESTROY MY HOUSE

WITH a guilty sense of my neglect, I recalled the old man and hurried back to him. He was still sleeping, and as I watched his peaceful face I was glad he had been spared the knowledge of what I had just seen. As for me, I had been so long unused to such things that I was sick and faint with the horror of Harry Forward's bloody act. And my feeling was the more intense when I reflected how averse Nicholson had been to meet him. Clearly, to his brother's magnanimity Harry owed his life, for until Nicholson had lost grasp of his temper he had had the best of it, and there was no time during the first few minutes and until he disarmed his adversary, when he could not have forced the other's guard and ended the matter. I hated Harry, little as I knew him, and as for Nicholson, I found myself warming to him again. Liar and plotter though I knew him to be, I thought with real grief on his downfall, and prayed he might be farther from his end than he had seemed. Indeed, I may as well say it here, there was a charm about the man that I have never been able to fully understand, and to this day I think of his case with pity and regret rather than with anger.

The chance remarks of the Colonel had convinced me that there was in his heart, too, a tender spot for the rebellious son, and I concluded that for the present I would say nothing about the scene I had just witnessed, but keep that bitterness from the old man's cup so long as I could.

He slept soundly, and I left him there and made my way back out of the woods to await developments from Forward House. And this time I sought a place which should command a more extensive view.

The point where I came out into the open was just at the crest of the hill and farther east than my old look-out, and it overlooked both Forward House and the road that passed my own dwelling. Beyond, I saw the dark waters of the open sea wrinkling in the morning breeze. There I stood and waited, and the first streak of sunlight fell upon a band of men stringing down the road to the sea. In their midst walked two with a litter, and I wondered whether Nicholson were dead or alive. The band moved swiftly; my spirits rose at the riddance, and I breathed more freely when I saw their haste.

But such consolation as I got from this was short-lived, for as they approached my house, I saw part of them strike off the road into the bushes, and the rest kept straight on and halted in a line at the front—all but the bearers of the litter, who kept on with their burden toward the Crag.

I knew that the men who had disappeared were reconnoitring for no good purpose, and I waited with a growing anxiety. I thought of the old man's warning and congratulated myself that I had heeded it—yet in the same breath I was wishing that Nicholson were himself there as leader, for I fancied he would have allowed no harm to come to me. There had been no noise, but after a few minutes of suspense I heard shouts, and at the same time the sailors in the road began running one by one into my grounds. I watched them until only three were left in the road, and then I saw what stopped my heart for a moment—a line of smoke curling up through the trees. The villains had fired my house !

93

Of what I did and said when the truth came to me, I have the most imperfect remembrance. I raved and swore and shook my fist impotently at my enemies. Dead or dying though he was, I called down all the curses of heaven upon the man I had taken in from the storm, and whose lawless crew was repaying me by burning the roof that had sheltered him. Indeed, for one fleeting moment there was murder in my heart when I thought of the old man behind me in the woods, through whom I had been brought to this pass. But I thank God that, even in my blind rage, I had enough of my reason left to be ashamed of this feeling as soon as I realized it.

It seemed to me that I stood there many minutes, though in reality I suppose the interval was measured by seconds, when something happened which overcame my rage, and left me staring in fright, horror, and amazement. I felt the earth quiver under my feet, I saw the air filled with fragments of wood and stone, and a sheet of red flame in the midst of it, and then came the sound of an explosion more terrible than any I had ever heard. Close upon its echoes followed the shrieks of wounded men, and out of the cloud of smoke and dust that settled where my house had stood, I saw three sailors running like frightened sheep down the road to the sea.

My first impulse was to hurry to the spot, but I checked myself and went back to Colonel Forward ; my first duty was to him. To my great surprise he was still sleeping soundly. His exhaustion had been too great to be stirred by what I thought must have shaken the world itself. I did not disturb him, but left him there and hurried across the fields to his house.

The place was deserted, to all appearances, though smoke still issued from the chimneys. I entered by a side door that stood ajar, and once inside, the mark of the vandal was every-where evident. Fires were smouldering on the hearths, and I saw they had been used to pre-pare food. Every bit of furniture capable of concealing a drawer, had been ransacked—the carpets and rugs had been started at the edges—pictures had been turned to the wall, and the paper backings of their frames ripped open—the upholstering of the chairs had been started, and everywhere the work showed a most thor-ough search for something, whether successful or not I could not tell. But it was not the work of ordinary robbers, for the heavy plate on the side-board in the dining-room was still there, though disarranged, and elsewhere in the house articles of intrinsic value, which must have appealed to the greed of a mere thief, were undisturbed.

I went quickly from room to room, and everywhere lay the same traces of confusion. But my discoveries terminated in the library, where every book had been taken from its shelf and the most painstaking search had clearly been made. The desk had been forced, and its papers lay in a confused heap on the floor. And while I looked on in amazement, forgetting for a moment the errand that had brought me there, I heard a moan from a little room that opened from the library and that I had not yet visited.

I hurried in, and there, in a row on the floor, lay four men bound and gagged. They were of the Colonel's party, of course, and the tally was complete save for their leader and Harry Forward. My eyes sought out the young man's second in that morning fight, and him I loosed. Without a word he set to work and helped me with the rest. They seemed none the worse for their experience, but each had heard the terrific explosion and plied me with questions as to its meaning. I sent the three off down the road to investigate, and kept the first man by me. When we were by ourselves, he turned upon me suspiciously.

"Before we go any further," said he, "I want to know what I'm dealing with. I saw you here last night, and your position was, to say the least, peculiar."

"I am John Hunt," I began.

"Damn your name," he interrupted impatiently, "I am Albert Lorimer, but what does that signify? I know who you are—you're the hermit from the cape, and I've seen you many a time—but what were you doing here with Dick Forward last night?—that's what I want to know."

"Put on your hat and come with me," said I. "I'll tell you as we go."

He did as I bade him, and as I hurried him down the road, I explained my position as well as I could. His face lightened as I went on, and as I finished, he stopped and held out his hand.

"They seem to have played tag with you, Mister Hunt," said he, with a smile, "but you've done the old man a good turn, and I'll shake hands. And now, whereabouts in the woods have you left him?"

"He's safe enough until we get back," said I. "I've told you my story, now tell me where is Harry?"

He started and looked keenly at me.

"What Harry?" said he, affecting surprise. "What the devil do you know of Harry?"

"I saw the fight this morning," said I, briefly.

He changed his manner in an instant.

"And the Colonel—does he know about it?" he asked, eagerly, and when I reassured him, "Then keep it to yourself," he added, with evident relief. "I'll tell you now that the old man loves Dick yet, and it would kill him if he knew what Harry had done for him. If we have to tell him anything, we can tell him a lie."

"But tell me," I asked. "Is Nicholson dead?"

"Nicholson?" he repeated, with a puzzled look. "Oh, you mean Dick Forward? I don't know. Yes, dead or dying."

I would have asked where they had left him, but we could talk no more, for the road was already filling with dazed and frightened fishermen from the village, and a party of them joined us.

We found a scene of wreck and ruin. My house was gone, and the trees that had stood nearest it lay prostrate on the ground. It did not seem possible that any human agency could have accomplished the havoc, but when I said as much to Lorimer, he gave me a curious look and shrugged his shoulders.

Of the house and of those who had been by it, there was literally nothing left, and I think this obliteration of the band struck me as the most awful part of the business. It would have been some relief to have any tangible evidence of what had happened. I knew that not less than eighteen or twenty men had been in or around the house at the instant of the explosion, and of all that crew it seemed that the three I had seen running had alone escaped. But the first feeling of horror which had possessed me, gave way to rage when I thought on the magnitude of my own loss, and what the villains had done for me. And I thought bitterly of the chief villain of all, and wondered whether he had gone with the rest.

The men from the village were exploring the grounds curiously, and there were wicked looks on the faces of the fellows from Forward House. Presently Lorimer came up to me.

" Don't turn quickly," he said, in a tone scarcely above a whisper ; " I can't answer for my men if they see him, but there's a black spot down the road that should be Dick Forward on his stretcher, where his cowardly men have left him. I'll keep my men busy, and set the fishermen to work, and do you slip quietly down and see whether I am right. If it is Dick, dead or alive, draw him under cover of the bushes out of sight. We must get him back to the house.''

I had forgotten all about the two men with the litter who had kept straight on past my house while their companions turned in, but Lorimer's first words brought the incident back to me, and as he led the crowd into the yard on a pretext of making further investigation, I turned away and started quietly down the road.

The dark object lay by the roadside, two or three hundred yards away, and as I got near it I saw it was the body of a man. It was Nicholson, as I knew before I came up to him, and a second glance showed me he was not dead, but unconscious.

At that instant all the devil in me was on top, and I stood and filled myself with the sight of him, and for the first minute my only sorrow was that he was not conscious of his plight. And with that I had sated my longing for revenge, I suppose, for I found myself making excuses for the scoundrel. In his state, it was more than likely that the attack on my house had been beyond his ken and will. And then my mind went back to that scene in the hollow, his manly bearing and his pluck; and I went on my knees beside him and called him by the name he had given himself.

He stirred at my voice. Then he opened his eyes and looked me full in the face, for I was bending over him. He stared blankly for a second, and something like a smile softened his drawn features.

"As I live," said he, weakly, "it's Mister Hunt! For the love of God, John Hunt, where did you drop from, and where am I?"

X

HE was but the shadow of the man whom I had seen striding vigorously across the fields hardly an hour ago. Weak and white, and with the mark of death on his face, he looked bravely back into mine and read my thoughts.

"You're well quit of a troublesome guest," said he, "for I'll sit no more at your table."

A shout from up the road broke in upon us; the villagers had come upon some ghastly relic in the ruins. The sound quickened my senses to the situation, and I was surprised that the dying man noticed it also.

"What was that?" he asked, peevishly, "and what am I lying here in the road for? Where's Allison—where are my men?"

"It's all right," I answered, soothingly. "I'm here to do you a service, but you mustn't ask any questions. Do as I tell you, and trust me. Now set your teeth together, for I've got to move you."

As tenderly as I could, I drew him back into the bushes away from the road. He looked at me wonderingly.

"Now," said I, "I've got to leave you, and it's all your life's worth and more too, to be seen here. Mind you lie still until I send the men for you."

"There's no fear about that," he whispered. "I'll be still enough before you get back. Oh, I know," he added, as I tried to look incredulous, "and so do you. I'm dying, Mister Hunt, and I've got daylight in both lungs. Can't you see the blood, man?"

"Who did it?" I asked, at a loss for a more sensible question.

"Excuse me," he said, feebly. "Between gentlemen, you know. Fair thrusts—both of them. If you've anything to do, you'd much better leave me and do it." And then closing his eyes, he said, softly to himself, "If I could see my father and Molly—just a minute, just a minute."

I turned away, and he mistook the cause.

"I say," he whispered, "is that all? No good-by or blessing or anything? It's not far off."

And indeed I was of the same opinion as I looked at him, and I saw that if anything were

to be done, there was no time to lose. I took
his hand.

"I will say good-by if you wish it," said I,
"but I shall see you again, for I'm coming
back soon."

And without looking at that gray face again,
I turned and left him.

Lorimer was looking for me when I got back
to the scene of the wreck, and he drew me
aside.

"It is Dick?" he asked, with a scowl.

"Yes," said I, "and all but dead."

He hesitated a minute.

"It comes hard," he said, finally, "but the
old man would want it so. I'll do what I can.
Run along and look after the Colonel. Don't
tell him anything, but keep him there in some
way until you hear me calling to you. Now
tell me where I shall find you."

I told him as nearly as I could, and hurried
on to find the old man.

Events had chased so closely on each other's
heels that morning, that I had scarcely thought
of the woman who had inadvertently let me
into this adventure; but as I walked back to
Forward House on my way to the woods, I recalled Nicholson's words, and wondered where
the girl was. From the slight speech that had

passed between the brothers before they tried
conclusions, I divined the cause of Harry's
hate, and the girl's position to the other. She
should be Richard's wife, and even now was
probably awaiting his return to her — but
where? I reached the top of the hill and
stopped a moment for breath, and as I turned
to look back down the road, my question was
answered, for a mile or two off shore a black
steamer was coursing north. She was the only
moving thing on all that sweep of sea, and my
eyes followed her eagerly until, with a broad
turn, she came about and went slowly back
south. I was positive that here was the yacht
that had brought the invaders, but I had no
time to watch her further, and turning my back
to the sea, I hurried on to Forward House.

I had had no thought of stopping there, but
as I passed the side door which had given entrance to me earlier in the morning, I heard a
sound inside the house and instantly divined
its meaning. The Colonel had returned, and
when I had passed in and through to the library, I found him standing in the middle of
the room, gazing sadly on the ruin about him.
He glanced toward me as I entered.

"See what they have done to me," he said.

"They've done far worse for me," I answered, sorrowfully, "and worse than either for themselves."

"What do you mean?" he asked, sharply. And then as if the question brought him back, "Where have you been, Mister Hunt—and where are my men?"

"You have heard nothing?"

"No, no," he said, impatiently. "How the devil should I hear anything?"

Ordinarily I should have shown temper at his brusqueness, but when I thought of the misery still in store for him, I had no anger left, and I told him what had happened to my house and the fellows who had fired it. He turned white when I came to the catastrophe.

"Good God," said he, "what folly! What can Dick have been thinking of? He was not there, Mister Hunt; depend upon it, he was not there. He knows the danger of the stuff too well. There was an accident, you may be sure of that—and yet I cannot see why he should take it into your house at all."

"I don't know what you are driving at," said I, "but if you think it was an accident that set my house afire, I know better," and I told him how I had watched the villains go coolly to their work.

"Oh, as to that," he answered, unconcernedly, " they meant that much, I dare say—but the explosion—pshaw ! They wouldn't have wasted the stuff in that way."

He was talking riddles to me, and that and his cool indifference to my own misfortune maddened me in spite of myself.

" Have you no thought but of yourself? " I cried, angrily. " While you are dwelling on your own miserable secret and keeping me in the dark, remember the position I am in and the outrage I have suffered. Is it nothing to you that through taking up your cause my house and everything I owned have been swept away? "

" Tut," he answered, peevishly, and I saw the son in his look and gesture. " That's a great pity, of course, but suppose you had been in your house. Rather go down on your knees and thank God and my warning that you are not lying over ten acres of ground this minute ! And instead of that," he went on with a little sigh, " it has been your privilege to see the first practical test of the most powerful explosive on earth ! "

I looked at him with a growing pity. The man was clearly mad ; and while that thought was passing, his brave front vanished and the tears were trickling down his face. So while

I could have killed him for his indifference to
me in one instant, the next my soul was melt-
ing for him. And all this time a dozen differ-
ent trains of thought were tramping through my
head, and with them marched that preposter-
ous story of the wretched son, in which I now
saw the thread of truth—a story so skilfully
built upon to enlist my sympathy, and to cover
the villainy of the man's purpose. I saw his
vile heart laid bare, I saw him as he was, a
mercenary plotter against his own blood, a
man who had painted his father a thief and a
liar to enlist me in his own outrageous cause—
but what cause? And a vision of the girl
trooped after him, the girl with her fear and
misery, her stealth and haste, and all for what?
And then that picture of the old man running
through the darkness, and digging like a savage
in the woods, and crying out that it was gone
—what?

I wonder now that I could have been so
dense, but God made me somewhat slow of
comprehension, and I had not looked for so
much hell in so trifling a thing as that bottle.
But the truth came to me somehow in the
midst of my jumbled thoughts.

" Oh, you fool," I groaned.

The Colonel looked at me in surprise, and

108

his eyes seemed singularly clear for a mad man's.

"I am wondering where my wits have been," said I, answering his look. "I left one of your infernal powder bottles in my library last night."

He looked puzzled, but whatever answer he would have made me never came, for in the same instant we both heard voices and the sound of men in the front hall. There was a rough tread, and a scuffling of feet as of men bearing a heavy burden, and as we listened, Lorimer's voice broke upon us.

The Colonel looked relieved and started for the door, but I detained him, for I knew the sight that awaited him.

They had not reckoned on finding the old man here, and it was Richard Forward they were bringing home. I knew this and blocked the Colonel's path.

"I would not go," said I, earnestly. "Stay this side the door and let me talk to you."

He looked at me in amazement.

"You forget yourself," said he, stiffly. "Stand aside."

And in the instant that we stood there—he calmly waiting, and I uncertain—Lorimer's voice broke the silence and bore us this cruel speech.

"Lay him here," says he. "He's as well here as anywhere, and he'll never feel a bed again."

And then the door behind me opened, and Lorimer stood face to face with the Master of Forward House.

The old man drew himself up.

"Is it Dick or Harry?" he asked, sternly; but he got his answer from beyond and in a voice I knew.

"Father, father," and it was the echo of Nicholson's strong voice that I heard, "I'll not stay long, but I want to start clean;" and as the old man went trembling from our sight, the rest trooped out and left the two together, and I heard him sobbing his forgiveness as the door closed upon them.

For some minutes, Lorimer scarcely noticed me, but stood at the window scowling. Finally he turned and abruptly dismissed the two men who had remained in the room with us, and when they had gone, he strode impulsively up to me, and laid a hand on each of my shoulders.

"Mister Hunt," says he, bringing his face level with mine and looking me squarely in the eyes, "this is a bad business, and I wish we were all quit of it—but that dying man in there with all his sins is a man—do you hear me—a *man!*"

He paused, and I waited for him to go on.

"And as for Harry," he continued, "I hope he's in hell this minute, where he belongs. I've talked with Dick since you left him, and he's badly off and going fast, but he made me promise not to tell the old man about that affair with Harry, and all for Harry's sake, mind you!"

He gripped me with his two hands as he spoke, and his eyes reddened.

"Well?" said I.

"Well," he blurted out, and fairly shook me, "that's a man's part, I say. But what's more, he spoke of you—*you*—and says he: 'Do you straighten things with John Hunt, Lorimer, for I'll not see him again, and he did me a good turn.'"

And with that the man flung his hands to his face and turned again to the window. I respected his feeling and looked away. He wheeled around and faced me after a moment.

"And that," said he, resuming, "is what I

shall do. I've promised him and he deserves it. How much do you know already?"

"Nothing," said I, and at that he looked me over in astonishment.

"There's no joke about this," said he, gruffly. "I'm keeping faith with a dying man, and I don't want any nonsense with you."

"I tell you," said I, stiffly, "that I know nothing about this—I don't care to urge the point."

"I beg your pardon," he answered, rather more graciously, "but surely—the Colonel's invention?"

I feigned not to see the incredulity that filled his face.

"And what," said I, "is that?"

He looked at me so long without replying that I felt my color rising.

"You will bear in mind, Mister Lorimer," said I, "—if that's your name—that I'm no neighborhood gossip. Your and your master's business——"

He raised a deprecating hand.

"I am sorry," said he, "and I was wrong to doubt you. But I appreciate your kind, Mister Hunt, rare as it is. Believe me, in my gospel there's nothing so lovable as an indifferent neighbor! And now I've more to tell you than I thought—and we'd better go outside.''

And as we walked across the fields together, he told me what I shall relate in his own words as far as memory will indulge me.

XI

LORIMER EXPLAINS

"I HAVE lived here five years," Lorimer began, " and next after his own blood, no one knows the old man as well as I. When he left the service, he brought me back here to live with him, and for a long time I was his only companion. I don't know how to explain my position, unless you choose to call me a sort of superintendent—and that doesn't fill the bill, for he has made both friend and confidant of me.

"You see his wife had recently died, and his two sons, Dick and Harry, were long out of leading strings and in their own ways. Harry was in the army and Dick in the navy, but they were both inordinately lazy, and when they came into a little money at their mother's death, Dick threw up his commission outright, and Harry did even worse: he got into bad ways and was shortly sent home.

"Now, all this time the old man was working

on an idea that had furnished both the pleasure and the business of his life for many years. Ten years ago he conceived the invention of that infernal powder which lies at the bottom of the whole business, and he's done little but experiment with the devilish stuff since.

" I think it was a fear that Harry would surprise his secret, that made the old man so mad with the boy when he came home. At any rate, he sent the young fellow packing in short order, and went on more stolidly than ever with his experiments. Dick, meanwhile, did not interfere with the Colonel, for he never came home at all, and neither son at this time took the old man's occupation seriously.

" But shortly after Harry's dismissal there was a change in the establishment here: An old army friend of the Colonel died, leaving a daughter — poor and without a relative on earth—and the old man, out of the goodness of his heart, brought her here to live. If you've ever seen Molly Bridgman, you needn't be told what a fine woman she is. The Colonel got very fond of her, and before long she was sharing honors with the invention in occupying his time—though I think the powder always held first place.

" About two years ago, Harry appeared on

the scene again, and this time the father took him in. The boy had run through his money and came home looking like a tramp. He had no sooner been taken back than he dropped his humility, and became as overbearing as ever. He was a disagreeable fellow—gave himself great airs, kept the Colonel in a stew most of the time, and fell head over ears in love with Miss Bridgman ; then he sulked and took to drinking because she would have none of him. I can't begin to tell you the trial he was to the old man, who was meanwhile making very substantial progress with his experiments, and who had to conduct everything in absolute privacy because he so distrusted Harry. He talked with me about it, and finally he wrote to Dick and told him how matters stood, and Dick came home.

"How much the Colonel told him about the invention, I don't know — but it was enough to arouse Dick's interest, at any rate. He stayed a month, and after he had gone, the old man kept up a correspondence with him— a thing he had not done for years.

"All this made Harry wild with jealousy. He probably suspected more than there really was, for the Colonel was canny enough with the nearest of us.

" So Harry set to work to undermine Dick's influence with his father, and he played his first card a year ago, when Dick came on a second visit. He pretended to be delighted to see Dick again, gained his confidence while he was here, and played his game so neatly that Dick interfered on his behalf with the Colonel. Then when Dick had gone away again, Harry ran to the old man with a cock-and-bull story about having surprised a scheme of Dick's to swindle the father out of his rights —and the whelp urged that Dick's intercession with the old man was only intended as a bribe to keep Harry's mouth shut. I don't know the whole story, but I'm sure it wouldn't have worked with Colonel Forward if another thing hadn't come to his knowledge at the same time. He surprised a correspondence going on between Miss Molly and Dick, and found that the son had been making love to his ward, and that they had kept their own counsel in the matter.

" Now, the Colonel's notions of honor are rather strait-laced, and it annoyed him that Dick should have concealed anything of the sort from him, so he wrote a sharp letter, and it came out that Harry had been tale-bearing and there was hell to pay right off.

"Perhaps other things were at work with the Colonel—I don't know as to that. There seemed something a bit shady about Dick, and his reticence gave color to the suspicion. All we knew of him during his absences was that he was 'following the sea' as he explained to us, and that left a wide range for conjecture.

"At any rate, the Colonel's suspicious nature had got a shock, and he lost confidence in Dick, and when Dick came back here in high feather, about a month ago, to renew his business negotiations about the invention, the old gentleman stood him off and politely declined to have anything to say about the matter. Dick pocketed the insult and went away, but he left the old man uneasy, and at Harry's suggestion our establishment here was increased, and we began to maintain something like military discipline about the place. More than that, the Colonel suddenly suspended work, and removed all traces of it. I'm sure I don't know where he carried his stuff, but it was taken away from the house.

"I don't know whether the Colonel heard from him again or not, but the next chapter of the business that I have any knowledge of, was Dick's appearance here day before yesterday. He was as pleasant as though nothing had

happened, and told us he had run down to say
good-by, as he was going out of the country
next day. The Colonel met him half-way, and
whatever talk they had in private, seemed to
have settled any difference that lay between
them. I thought that Harry was of that
opinion, too, for he made no great effort to
conceal his annoyance at Dick's return. Peace
seemed quite restored for everyone but him,
and even Miss Molly looked brighter at dinner
than I'd seen her for many a day. But Harry
sat sullen and frowning.

"As we got up from table, the Colonel
turned to him.

" ' Harry,' says he, ' your brother's going
away to-morrow on a long trip.'

" ' Dear me,' sneered Harry. ' I'm sorry
for that ! '

"I saw Dick bite his lip, but the old man
affected not to notice anything.

" ' Come into the library,' said he. ' I
want to talk to you and Dick together.'

" ' I'm sorry,' Harry said, with a queer look
at his brother, ' but I'm busy this evening, and
you'll have to excuse me.'

" He whipped off by himself after that, and
when I walked out under the trees five minutes
later, he was standing under the library win-

dow and puzzling over a letter which he held
so the light from the house fell upon it—and
he shoved it hastily into his pocket as I came
up, and went into the house. A minute later,
I saw a light shining from his window in the
top of the house.

"My own room here is in the second story
over the library, and the Colonel and Dick
slept on the first floor. I went up early, and
for a long time I heard the murmur of steady
talking below. I could not tell the voices, but
from what had passed at dinner, I knew they
should be those of the Colonel and Dick.

"About midnight, the sound stopped; then
doors closed, and the house became still. But
I had hardly got quiet when I heard Miss
Bridgman's door at the end of the passage
creak, and an instant after someone went softly downstairs. A dead silence followed—and
then a sound directly below me in the library
—then heavier footsteps, a woman's faint cry
—a slamming door, and then voices.

"I sprang out of bed and opened my door.
The Colonel was talking excitedly in the library.

"'She was at my papers,' he was saying.
'What mischief is this?'

"'My dear father,' Dick answered, calmly,

'I assure you I know no more about it than you. I heard the noise, and like yourself, I came in to investigate.'

"'And how is it you are dressed at this hour?' the Colonel asked, suspiciously.

"'I had not undressed,' replied Dick. 'Really, father, your manner is most unpleasant,' and he spoke in an injured tone. 'I assure you I see no sense in all this, and as I told you to-day, Miss Bridgman is no longer anything to me.'

"I heard the Colonel growl out some reply as he crossed the library, and went swiftly through the hall to the other side of the house.

"'Well?' Dick called after him, and I thought rather nervously, 'where are you going?'

"The old man had reached a window.

"'There she goes,' he shouted. 'There's her light out on the road.'

"I had slipped out to the head of the stairs, and as Dick passed the foot in pursuit of the old gentleman, he was cursing at someone's stupidity softly under his breath, and I drew my own conclusions. The old man was fumbling at the door-fastenings as Dick came up with him.

"'Stop,' said the younger man, persuasively. 'Wait a bit. Where's Harry all this time? Before you go any further, let's see where we are.'

"'What do you mean?' the Colonel shouted.

"'Do you remember his excuses at dinner?' said Dick.

"I did, at any rate, and I remembered his secrecy about the letter he had been reading when I came upon him in the yard. I began to wonder which of the sons was at the bottom of it all.

"'Go to Harry's room and see if he's there,' Dick continued. 'I'll lay you a little bet——'

"I didn't hear the rest, for I bolted back into my own room as the Colonel came tearing up the stairs, and an instant later I heard him at Harry's door. He was back again in a breath and had joined Dick in the hall.

"'Well?' asked the son, coolly.

"'The traitor,' said his father, 'he's gone, too!'

"'Then do you stay here, and let me follow them,' said Dick, quickly, and he unbolted the door. They passed out together, and down the drive.

"I waited for an hour with my door ajar,

and then I heard steps approaching the house.
A key was put cautiously into the lock of the
side door, and a man entered the house. I recognized Harry's nervous step as he walked
through to the library, and his voice as he
gave a short exclamation of surprise at what he
saw there. The next moment he had gone to
his father's room, and to Dick's, and was upstairs at a jump and into mine without ceremony.

"'Lorimer,' he said, groping his way to my
bed and fumbling for me; 'Lorimer, what in
hell does this mean? Get up, man, and tell
me what's happened.'

"I made no excuses for being half-dressed,
but got up and told him what I had heard, and
when I finished, he bade me go downstairs
with him, and we got into the hall just in time
to see the Colonel come in at the front door
with a lantern in his hand. He heard us on
the stairs and looked up, and when he saw
Harry, he nearly dropped his lantern in amazement.

"'Harry,' said he, aghast, 'Harry, Harry!'
And while he stood with his mouth open, Harry
fished a bit of crumpled paper out of a pocket,
and thrust it in his face.

"'Read that,' said he, triumphantly.

"The Colonel recovered himself, and lifting his lantern, smoothed the paper and read aloud:

" 'If Harry Forward wants evidence of his brother's treachery to him and to his father, let him come to the old hotel at East Crag at 12 to-night and ask for Mr. Allison. He may be able to frustrate a great fraud if he will heed this warning from one who wishes both him and his father well.'

"The old man looked it over carefully, and turned a wicked look upon his son.

" 'Where did you get that?' he asked.

" 'It was brought over in the mail this after-noon,' said Harry.

" 'And you went, I suppose?' the old man continued.

" 'Yes,' replied the other, with manifest un-easiness, 'and I've done a good job, too, for I've seen the man——'

"The Colonel stopped him.

" 'You're a poor fool, Harry,' said he. 'That note was written on my own paper, with my own ink, in my own library—and it's a woman's hand. Unless I'm much mistaken, Molly wrote that herself, and Dick was prob-ably hanging over her shoulder when she did it!'

"For a moment Harry didn't seem to un-

derstand, then he started for the door without
a word.

" ' No,' said the old man, seizing his arm.
' You've done enough for one night, now stay
here. I want you,' and Harry slunk back.

" ' They've duped us to-night,' the Colonel
went on, ' and if Molly hadn't been too eager,
she might have found something valuable. As
it is, the papers are safe, and the samples they
can never find.' "

Lorimer stopped and shook his head.

" But the old man was wrong about that,"
he sighed, and paused a minute.

" Well," he resumed, " the old man sent
Harry upstairs to bed, and then we talked it
all out together.

" ' They'll be after us to-morrow,' says he,
' for the girl ran to the Crag, and Dick's evidently got a ship and some help off there. So
we'll just get our men and our house in fight-
ing trim, and give them a reception when they
come.'

" The next morning—that was yesterday—
he sent the three women servants away to the
town—for he said we'd have no petticoats on
the premises 'till the row was over. Lord
knows what excuse he made them—but they
know his ways."

He stopped and looked at me expectantly. But I was waiting for him to go on.

"Well?" he said, after a moment, driving his hands into his trousers pockets and stopping short in his walk.

"Are you done, then?" I asked.

"Yes," said he, and I thought uneasily. "Isn't there enough?"

"Too much or too little—as you please to look at it," said I, frankly. "I tell you, Mister Lorimer, you disappoint me. I make no question of the truth of what you say, and it explains much that has puzzled me. But you're keeping something back. There's not enough yet to account for what's happened."

As I spoke, I had turned at his lead and we were retracing our way to the house.

"I have told you all I may," says he, doggedly, "and my discretion is exhausted. If there's more behind it, it's none of my affair and much less yours. And if I were you, Mister Hunt, I'd be content with such explanation as lay in my way."

There was a harsh emphasis in his voice, and ' I said no more, but my wits were busy with surmises. We entered the house in silence, and as we passed into the library the Colonel was just appearing from the hall.

XII

THE ADVENT OF MISTER HAWK

I NEVER think of that straight figure in the doorway, without a pang of pity for the grief that lay upon his drawn face as he looked at us. I heard my watch tick as we waited for him to speak, and presently Lorimer walked over to him. The Colonel looked him through as he approached, and there was that in the old man's face that set the younger trembling and made his eyes shift.

"Lorimer," said he, "God forgive me, I have done wrong! But I did not know the truth!"

And as the other made no answer, he went on.

"You've been near to me in time past," says he, "now tell me this: Is there any blood on your hands?"

Lorimer seemed relieved at the manner of the question, and looked the Colonel squarely in the face.

"No," said he. "As I stand here, I had no part in it."

"And perhaps you can tell me," says the old man, trembling, "where is Harry Forward?"

But Lorimer's eyes drooped at that, and he shook his head.

"And I thank heaven that you cannot," said the Colonel, so I knew he at least suspected the truth.

He asked no more questions, but passed across to me.

"Mister Hunt," said he, and held out his hand, "you did not know my son Richard— you knew one Nicholson who lived a night and a day, and where he came from, God alone may tell. But of him who lies in there, nothing but good, nothing but good. He died like the brave man he was, and by the grace of his Maker he has gone where brave men go."

He turned away with his voice breaking, but pulled himself proudly together in the next breath.

"Lorimer," said he, "I shall carry out his wishes to the letter, and if God is good to me, I shall bring her back. Meanwhile do you and Mister Hunt watch here in my stead, for I trust you both."

128

And with no more words he left the room and we heard him pass out of the house. Then, by a common impulse, Lorimer and I turned to the hall.

There was no need to look twice at the stiff figure and the sunken face, to see that Richard Forward's business was done. From his appearance and the pathetic effort that had been made to compose the dead man's limbs and features, I judged the change had come some time ago. How long his father had stayed there with him after life had gone, we could not tell, but the clothes had been tenderly smoothed and the body looked as if already prepared for burial.

Together we lifted the stretcher, and carried the body to the room that had been Dick's, and laid him on his own bed. As I was opening the window shutters, I heard the clatter of horses' hoofs, and Colonel Forward and one of his men rode past on their way out of the grounds.

At that sound Lorimer pushed past me to the window, and stood looking down the drive. And as he watched the receding figure of his master, his eyes shone with excitement. Presently he drew back and turned again to me.

" I wonder at his hardihood," said he.

"His years sit light enough when there's a man's work to do."

"He seems a brave old gentleman," I ventured.

"You may well say that," said he, "but he needs it all this day, and may he be put in the way of what he seeks."

"And that?" I asked.

"And that," says he after me, "is first of all — forgiveness;" and suddenly fell silent again with his face to the window, and began crying softly like a girl.

I would have left him then, but he called on me to stay—and when he had pulled himself together, he followed me from the room.

But that excursion to the dead man's room had sapped his nerve. He stuck at my elbow in the passageway, and gave the dark corners a wide berth and a furtive glance as we passed.

He drew a deep breath of relief when we got back to the library.

"I'm for a drink," says he, "and if you'll be persuaded?"

He brought two glasses and a bottle of whiskey, and in some tedious fashion the forenoon wore away, and when the sunlight began creeping in at the western windows we were still there.

Lorimer sat the greater part of the while sunk in a sullen study, and with a great and growing irritation at my attempts to stir him. Twice, indeed, I had essayed to leave the room, but each time he had detained me. And as I got on my feet for the third time,

" For God's sake," said he, impatiently, " sit down and stay where you are. Do you think I'm sticking here without a method ? "

He pulled out his watch and sat frowning at it.

" They'll be here soon," said he, " or I'll know they have sailed away with a very stiff old gentleman—and if that is so, God stay by him in such hands."

He had scarcely spoken when a distant sound caught his ear and he listened attentively. Then he got up with a sigh of satisfaction and passed across to the window. A moment after I was beside him, at his call, and together we watched three visitors coming up the drive. Well in the van was the Colonel's man afoot, and behind him, on his own and his master's horses, rode two strange men. They were a good deal muffled for the day, I thought, but one of them, in particular, attracted my notice by the studied concealment of his face. He wore a soft felt hat pulled well down over his forehead, a great pair of green goggles at his eyes, and a coarse black beard and mustache that covered the lower part of his face.

When the trio had reached the point opposite us, this man swung himself from his horse and approached the house alone. Lorimer met him on the threshold of the side door.

" You are Mister Lorimer ? " the stranger asked, brusquely.

" I am," says my companion, bluntly, " and I could give you a name if I didn't sicken at thought of what it should be."

But if the other was dashed at this impudence, he made no sign.

" Never mind," said he, contemptuously, " I come from a very civil old gentleman whose example is lost upon his servants, it seems. Show me the room."

" By what authority ? " asked Lorimer, quite white with anger, but got no further, for the stranger was chuckling behind his beard, which flopped from side to side as he moved.

" You waste time," says he, at length, " and you only prolong your master's discomfort. Take me where that dead man is—if you've such a thing on the premises. Don't be a fool, Mister Lorimer, and let's get the business done with."

Lorimer wheeled about to me.

"Come with us," he commanded, and passed out of the room. The stranger did not once glance my way, and I fell in behind them.

We entered Dick's room in the same order, and Lorimer went straight to the bed and pulled down the sheet that covered the dead man's face.

"You may cover him again," said the stranger, coolly, after a glance. "I am satisfied."

All this time he had not removed his hat, but the cause was so manifest that I had scarcely noticed it as a rudeness, and I thought Lorimer was no more awake to resenting it than I. And as the man turned from the bed, he faced me for the first time, and on the instant sprang back with a little cry. It was the impulse of a man suddenly startled beyond self-control, and a second afterward he was as indifferent as you please. But the action was not lost upon Lorimer, who looked keenly at each of us in turn, and my own surprise was not less than his.

"You've met a friend," says he to our guest, sneeringly ; and then to me, "Do you know him, Mister Hunt?"

At my name the man started again, and

though I shook my head in reply to Lorimer's question, something in the stranger's manner sent a shiver of apprehension down my spine. As for him, he was plainly demoralized at the incident, and he concealed his agitation only lamely. He started for the door without further ceremony, but Lorimer quickly blocked his way.

"It may be against orders," said he, grimly, "but by God, you shan't leave the room till you've shown your face to us. Off with that trumpery!" and as the fellow made no sign of complying, Lorimer strode up to him, and with the quickness of a cat, ripped off the soft hat, the green goggles, and lastly the coarse false beard that hid his face. And in the shock of that disclosure I stood aghast, for, naked of disguise, stood a man whose name had not been on my lips and whose face I had not looked upon for more than twenty years. And if you ask me who he was, it serves my present purpose to say no more of him than this: He had been my friend and I had been his in that earlier time, and chance had drifted us apart. In the light of what I was to learn before he left Forward House, I could wish that the same chance had kept our paths divergent to the end. But in the moment that we faced each other,

youth touched my heart, and the years he had
been lost to me were as nothing.

When he saw the look in my face, the anger
melted in him, and he paid no heed to Lorimer. He came on with outstretched arms.

"John," said he, impulsively, "I had not
thought to see you again. Will you touch the
unclean thing I am, for old times' sake? Believe me, this is when a man's sins are hell to
him."

And for answer my hands were on his shoulders. I had not said a word, when Lorimer,
who was watching us with amazement, threw
back his head with a boisterous laugh.

"So you've found a friend, Mister Hawk,"
says he. "Well, you drop in soft places, but
you'll drop on nothing, one of these days, and
that will surprise both your heels and your
neck."

My hands fell to my sides again, and I took
a step back. I stared at them both, and Lorimer read my look.

"What," says he, "you don't know him,
then? 'The Hawk,'" he added, with a slight
emphasis; and I took another step back, for in
my day the mention of that name in my part of
the world made goose-flesh of a brave man, and
pulp of a coward. No outlaw on land or sea

carried such terror to lonely places as "The Hawk," and it was a fortune to any man who should bring him in sight of a jail. But who he was or had been, none knew, and even among his men, it was said, he was known only as "Mister Hawk." These things I knew, but that I had lived to throw my arms about him and welcome him as the dearest friend of my life, left me stupid with astonishment.

"You," said I, stammering, "'The Hawk?' No, no, Mister Lorimer, you're mistaken. This man is——"

But the visitor raised his hand and voice in protest.

"You are both right," said he, wearily, "I am 'Mister Hawk' to all but you, John Hunt, and that other name you and I will keep between us. It has slipped from me with every other good thing, long ago. And the only kindness you can do me now is to seal your lips upon it for the sake of those who have forgotten me."

The man has long since passed to his reckoning after the disgraceful manner of his kind, but the name that halted on my lips that day has never since passed them, and never shall.

We went back to the library, Lorimer still dazed, and Mister Hawk threw himself into a chair. He seemed to have quite recovered his coolness.

"Mister Lorimer," said he, jauntily, "my attitude means weariness. It is customary among gentlemen——"

"Take it," said Lorimer, gruffly, handing him the bottle and pushing a glass across the table; "take it—but excuse me!"

"You'll not drink with me?" says Mister Hawk, with the air of one much hurt. "As you please, man, but you're the loser. I've heard of your master's liquors before this."

But Lorimer got up in dudgeon and stalked out of the room, slamming the door after him.

"A surly fellow," said the other, easily, and poured himself a drink. His manner repelled me, and I was beginning to regret my impulsive welcome of him. He saw the change and it sobered him.

"Hunt," said he, "until ten minutes ago I had thought myself beyond the touch of a good impulse, and here I find myself dumb in your presence lest I add your loathing to the rest of my burden. Let us think of what I was—not what I am."

"God knows I have no wish to read you a lecture," said I. "I am helpless at the absurdity of the situation. I cannot square the man I knew with the monstrous villain that rumor makes you."

He flushed a little and laughed uneasily.

"You're damned lavish of words," said he, with some show of irritation. "There aren't many men who'd call me a 'monstrous villain' to my face."

"And fewer yet," I answered, tartly, "who would own your friendship before a witness."

"There's something in that," he answered, dryly. "'Auld lang syne' allows an extravagance of expression—both ways."

The truth is, that left alone, we were both uncomfortable and embarrassed—and I was glad when he presently said he must be off; yet there was something I ached to ask him—and he gave me an opening.

"Hunt," said he, "I shall always regret it hereafter if I don't give you a chance to tell me how you happen here and what you are doing."

So I gave him a digest of the day and a half, much as I have set it down here, and he heard me through to the end.

"And now that you've made the move," said I, "I'll tell you that I'm travelling on the outskirts of this business—and you can clear it up."

His whole manner changed.

" Be advised," said he, seriously, " and stay on the outskirts."

" Is that quite disinterested, Mister Hawk ? " I asked—and he was silent for a minute or two.

" My lieutenant was Richard Forward," said he, " and I'll say no more than that."

" I had guessed that much," I answered. " What was the woman's rank ? "

He set his glass upon the table.

" No more of that," he growled, and with a look that made me shiver at his possibilities. " If you're fool enough to be travelling on that line, I'm bound to set you right. I never saw the girl before last night, but I'll hear no harm of her. Now ask your questions, and I'll be frank with you, for when I turn my back on Forward House to-day, I shall have seen the last of it and you. What do you want to know ? "

" What brought that man here on his lawless errand ? " I asked, stoutly.

He sat quite still for some minutes, as if weighing the whole matter. And then :

" He came, first of all," says he, quietly, " for his wife. And she knows nothing of his disgraceful deeds—and I know all." He stopped and hesitated before continuing. " He loved the woman and wanted to cut loose from the bad. That was what he wanted. Another man who knew these things, saw an advantage, and used it. So Richard Forward came for the fortune that lies in his father's secret, to buy his peace from those who held that knowledge over him. And he knew it was shame and exposure and degradation, and very likely death for him not to get it—because the other man owed him a grudge and was never known to show mercy to anyone.''

His voice was a whisper when he finished, and he evaded my eyes. But his meaning was so clear that I got up with a gesture of disgust.

'' 'Another man,' '' said I, quoting him. '' ' Another man '—and you're that other man. And you tell me that you have dropped as low as that ? ''

'' It's all in the point of view,'' he replied, with a sigh, '' I held the cards — and forced him.''

'' And you would have betrayed your own comrade,'' said I, '' and turned him over to the hangman if he hadn't done this thing ? ''

'' Excuse me,'' he answered, reddening, '' we need not go so far as that.''

'' As you please,'' I said, '' and I give you the benefit of a small doubt.''

" I'm afraid," said he, with an assumption of ease that his white face belied, " I'm afraid, Mister Hunt, that we've reached the fork of the road. I'm sorry I had to tell you, for I should like to leave you with a hand-shake, but never mind that, and see that you mind this : Molly Forward is never to know the truth, and if any man shall undeceive her, I'll——" he brought his fist down on the table with a crash. " As for me," he went on, ironically, " that you may think of me as badly as possible, I tell you I came here to-day to satisfy myself that Dick was not playing me a trick."

He got up, and with a hand that shook in spite of him, adjusted the grotesque disguises that Lorimer had torn from his face, and started for the door ; with his hand at the latch, he hesitated and turned back.

" Well—John ? " he asked.

" Go," said I, turning from him. " My eyes are tainted with the sight of you."

And with a little sigh, he passed out and I saw him no more, but presently I heard their horses on the drive.

XIII

I SAT there thinking of that strange interview until the room grew dark and Lorimer came in with a lighted lamp. And I have this to say for the man's delicacy—that neither then with his anger hot upon him, nor at any time afterward did he twit me with being Hawk's friend. He looked worn and anxious, and barely noticed my presence, but his eyes kindled at what he saw upon the table, and he picked up the glass that Mister Hawk had drunk from, and threw it from the window into the road. Then he fell to pacing the floor. I did not interrupt him, and he finally stopped before me.

"Hunt," he burst out with the thought that was uppermost in both our minds, "if he hadn't been under truce and with the Colonel and Molly aboard his vile ship, I'd have done for him here."

I made no comment, and he went on.

"Do you wonder," says he, "that I feared for the old man's safety in those hands? Do you wonder that I tremble when I think of him and Molly in the power of that villain?"

The man was so wrought upon by the suspense of waiting that I tried to reassure him, and I told him what the stranger had said of Molly. He was relieved at that, but as the evening wore away and nothing was heard from the pair, his nervousness returned. The clouds had gathered at nightfall, and a drizzling rain set in during the evening which added to our dreariness. About nine o'clock Lorimer left me, and I heard him talking with one of his men in the next room, and they shortly went out together.

I saw them from the window crossing the lawn with a lantern, and they disappeared in a clump of trees a little way from the house. But the blur of their light came through the rain to me, and I watched it there stationary for a long time.

While I was still looking at it, Lorimer came in alone. His rubber coat was blotched with mud, and he looked warm, but the anxious look had gone from his face and in its place there was excitement.

"They're coming," says he, eagerly; "and

now, Mister Hunt, you'll not take this amiss from me—all things considered?'' and picking up the lamp, bade me follow him.

He led me straight to Dick's room, and stopped by the bed.

'' It's the last time,'' he said, sorrowfully, and I understood him.

And when I turned away, he followed me from the room. But he took the lead once we were in the hall again, and instead of returning to the library, began ascending the stairs and bade me follow. He did not stop on the first landing, but kept on to the top of the house, and close on his heels I entered a bed-room at the end of the hall.

'' This will be your room,'' said he, lighting a candle on the dressing - table, and retiring quickly to the door. And before I could reply to him, he was gone and I heard his steps echoing down the long passage.

I was chagrined and disappointed, for I had hoped to see the Colonel's home-coming, and more than all else, to see her. But I was tired, too, and I went to bed and slept, and no sound was great enough in the house that night to disturb the heavy slumber that followed my exhaustion.

The sunshine in my face brought me out of

bed in the morning, and from my window I saw the sea, and no speck on its broad surface. While I stood looking there came a timid knock at my door, and a woman's voice followed it with the announcement of breakfast. And then I knew that order again reigned in Forward House ; but when the servants returned, or how, I do not to this day know.

I dressed and went downstairs. Lorimer was in the library and advanced upon me with a shining face.

"'They are come," said he, "and that chapter's done with, thank God ! Now let's get into the air, for there's one thing to show you yet, and a word or two to say besides—before you become one of the family."

I looked at him inquiringly.

"It's the old man's wish," said he. "You're to stay here anyway until your own house can be rebuilt."

I flushed a little.

"I'm not—— " I began, stiffly.

"Damn your pride," he broke in. "You've got to stay somewhere."

He seized my arm and hurried me from the room. When we got outside, he went on.

"And if he never speaks of this thing

145

again," said he, "it's his way, man—it's his way. Take him as he is."

He was leading me out through the trees, and presently we came to a knoll where the earth had been lately disturbed.

"And there lies Dick," says he, coming to a halt.

"Good God," said I, with a start. "And did you bury him like a dog, then?"

"Indeed," said he, with a show of spirit, "I've seen many as good a man as he go under with less ceremony—and few are so honestly mourned."

"But no rites," I urged. "No clergyman——"

"Excuse me," said he, dryly. "Have I then disguised myself so completely? I have taken holy orders myself, Mister Hunt, and I was the Colonel's chaplain for some years before he brought me here."

"You?" I exclaimed.

"I," he answered, but he reddened at the amazement in my voice. "And I see what sticks in your throat. But if I let slip an oath now and then—that's the most artificial of sins. It was all quite regular, Mister Hunt, I assure you. And now," he added with a sudden change of manner, "let me tell you another thing. I not only buried poor Dick last night, but I married him to Molly Bridgman, there in the library, three months ago. Before he died, Dick told his father of the marriage, but he would not tell who married them, and there are reasons why I am glad to leave the Colonel in ignorance for the present."

We had turned again to the house, and as we reached the door he held me back.

" One thing more," he said, "and this is for the good of us all. No word of Harry's part in this business has been dropped, but the old man is no fool. For his own sake, let Harry's name be forgotten. Never speak it before his father, and if I may ask as much for myself, never mention him to me. He is gone, and if I know him, he will not show his hateful face here again."

I did not see the Colonel until next day, and if I had reckoned on taking him up where I left him, my disappointment had been great. From that day to this, much as I have been with him, his speech has never touched upon that wretched time. But I stayed in his house for weeks, and though I have never forsworn the habits of a lifetime, which have made me a hermit, I got a great fondness for the brave old gentleman while I lived under his roof, and for Lorimer—but most of all for Molly Forward.

For some days after that night, she kept to her room, but when I entered the library one morning, perhaps a week later, I saw a woman standing before the fire. Her back was toward me, and I would have retreated, but she had heard me in the hall and turned at my entrance, and I stood face to face with Molly Forward. Every detail of that fair picture is stamped upon my mind to this day—the slender height of her graceful figure, more graceful for the rigid simplicity of the black gown and the absence of ornament—the refined face with its sensitive and delicate features—and the deep blue eyes, and the golden hair above it all. I thought then as I have thought since, that she was the loveliest woman I had ever seen.

She was quite alone as I entered the room, and I bowed clumsily and made as if to leave her; but she took a step forward and lifted a hand.

" You are Mister Hunt ? " she said, in the voice that had so thrilled me when I last heard it. " Pray do not go—I shall not wait for my father to present you," and she advanced and gave me her hand.

She showed no embarrassment—no sign of

consciousness that she had ever spoken with me before, and though I am little used to women, her gentle ways would have put a savage at his ease.

"Mrs. Forward," I began, and got no further. She was looking me frankly in the eyes, but at sound of my voice she turned her face away, and I felt the hand that lay in mine tremble. I said no more, for I knew what had come to her.

"You must forgive me," she said, after a moment's silence. "I am not very brave—and it is all so near. I was not sure—until you spoke."

And when she looked at me again, her eyes were brimming with tears.

So much for those with whom my lot was cast at that strange time, and with whom, please God, it shall be linked in some measure for all time to come. But of Harry, no vaguest word has ever reached me, and I choose to remember him as I last saw him—throwing his sword from him with that quick gesture of disgust, and striding away over the fields—for then, at least, I think he was sorry.

New Novels and Short Stories.

IN ATTRACTIVE UNIFORM BINDING.

❧

A POUND OF CURE.

A Story of Monte Carlo. By W. H. BISHOP. 16mo, $1.00.

A striking novel embodying a curious picture of the growth of the gambling spirit upon a young married man, whose only fault is his weakness in the presence of alluring pleasure. In addition to the very remarkable plot, the book is noteworthy for the delicate and picturesque descriptions of the scenery around Monte Carlo. Mr. Bishop's easy and very accurate English style adds to the effectiveness of the book as a work of art.

"A powerful and purposeful novel, clean and strong and interesting throughout."—*The Churchman.*

SALEM KITTREDGE,

And Other Stories. By BLISS PERRY. 16mo, $1.00.

Salem Kittredge is a story about a theological student, a pretty girl with active sympathies, and a young man addicted to drink. How these characters stood affected by each other during a season at Bar Harbor is told with much spirit and skill. The other stories are crisp and interesting, full of keen character drawing and a quick sense of human nature.

"Nine short stories, bright, dramatic, amusing, and forcibly written."—*Congregationalist.*

MARSENA,

And Other Stories. By HAROLD FREDERIC. 16mo, $1.00.

"Marsena" possesses, to a greater degree than perhaps anything Mr. Frederic has done, his perfection of local spirit and color, and the uncommon vividness with which he restores the feeling and situations of the war. There are four stories in the volume, all in Mr. Frederic's best vein.

"Capital tales, full of action and color."
—*Philadelphia Press.*

TALES OF THE MAINE COAST.

By NOAH BROOKS. 16mo, $1.00.

Including "Pansy Pegg," "The Apparition of Joe Murch," "A Hereditary Barn," "The Phantom Sailor," "The Waif of Nautilus Island," "A Century Ago," etc., all dealing with the romantic life of the people, and all full of local color.

"Highly interesting. Full of quaint humor."
—*Boston Beacon.*

A MAN WITHOUT A MEMORY,

And Other Stories. By WILLIAM HENRY SHELTON. 16mo, $1.00. *(Just Ready.)*

Chiefly stories of the Civil War in which the author was a soldier. Not only is the local color of the camp, march, and conflict vividly rendered, but the stories are related in a spirited and felicitous style that makes them as noteworthy for their literary form as for their substance.

A TRUCE,

And Other Stories. By MARY TAPPAN WRIGHT. 16mo, $1.00. *(Just Ready.)*

The range of Mrs. Wright's talent is remarkable, including tragic power and the lightness and vivacity of pure comedy. Her stories are varied in character, and reveal an unusual insight into human nature, and a literary style distinguished by equal force and charm.

FORWARD HOUSE:

A Romance. By WILLIAM SCOVILLE CASE. 16mo, $1.00. *(Just Ready.)*

Mr. Case is a new writer of striking individuality and of singular power, whose achievement in this book is in the highest degree noteworthy. It is a tale of stirring adventure dealing with the fortunes of the Forward family, told with a keen and true eye for dramatic effect and with a firm grasp of both character and scene—imaginative in structure and individual and racy in phrase. Indeed, the literary quality of the book is no less remarkable than the absorbing interest of the story.

Sold by all booksellers, or sent, post-paid, by

CHARLES SCRIBNER'S SONS, Publishers,

153-157 Fifth Avenue, New York City.